ARE YOU LISTENING?
LIFE IS TALKING TO YOU!

PHOEBE HUTCHISON

BALBOA.
PRESS
A DIVISION OF HAY HOUSE

www.areyoulistening.com.au

Balboa Press books may be ordered through booksellers or by contacting:

Balboa Press
A Division of Hay House
1663 Liberty Drive
Bloomington, IN 47403
www.balboapress.com.au
1 (877) 407-4847

Because of the dynamic nature of the Internet, any web addresses or links contained in this book may have changed since publication and may no longer be valid. The views expressed in this work are solely those of the author and do not necessarily reflect the views of the publisher, and the publisher hereby disclaims any responsibility for them.

The author of this book does not dispense medical advice or prescribe the use of any technique as a form of treatment for physical, emotional, or medical problems without the advice of a physician, either directly or indirectly. The intent of the author is only to offer information of a general nature to help you in your quest for emotional and spiritual well-being. In the event you use any of the information in this book for yourself, which is your constitutional right, the author and the publisher assume no responsibility for your actions.

Any people depicted in stock imagery provided by Thinkstock are models, and such images are being used for illustrative purposes only.
Certain stock imagery © Thinkstock.

Printed in the United States of America.

ISBN: 978-1-4525-1311-9 (sc)
ISBN: 978-1-4525-1312-6 (e)

Balboa Press rev. date: 3/4/2014

CONTENTS

People who understand the true nature of reality, those whom some traditions call enlightened, lose all sense of fear or concern. All worry disappears.—Deepak Chopra

PREFACE

The universe talks to us. The universe warns, inspires, and helps us on our journey on a daily basis. Often we don't realize we were being helped until we look back with our spiritual eyes.

I'd like to take you on a journey full of love, heartache, challenges, and accomplishments in the face of despair—this is your life. Through this journey you will come across characters who will teach you. Some will bring you pain, some will bring you joy, and some will help you learn more about yourself—but all will teach you wisdom. And while we all experience hard times, it is not these times we should focus on. We must decode the important lessons that lie beneath. Life is the most exquisite journey, and you must boldly follow the beat of your own drum, even though you may no longer hear it. Some people wander around with seemingly empty souls, serving the goals of others. Yet when you stand back and see your purpose, your life will become magical, enjoyable, and abundant. *You are unique.*

Acknowledge the power of your mind and follow your passions with the utmost dedication. Love what you do, where you live, and who you choose to spend time with. Start noticing the magical senses you have that help you stay on your most fulfilling life path. Be aware that darkness is not in you but is all around. Avoid darkness, and avoid the addictions that will bring darkness into your life. Follow the rules of success and mankind, and have unmovable faith that the universe is your servant; the universe will assist you to achieve almost anything you can imagine. Karma is real. While you cannot see every detail of life with your eyes, what happens to you is no mystery. You will be able to identify the many paths to destruction, so you can turn around and run the other way.

Every action and every thought has consequences. Sometimes it takes the universe a while to catch up. Your thoughts are possibly the most important part of your life. So why not have a little strategy? Know what you must do in order to have what you want.

As part of the research for this book, I have spoken with and studied a variety of people and researched psychological, self-help, and physics concepts. I have studied the lost and the successful, the rich and the poor, and the happy and the miserable in an effort to understand the connection between the mental and the physical. I discovered how our mind patterns, intuition, habits, psychological concepts, rules of life, cultures, coincidences, genetics, quantum physics, and the unseen energies of the supernatural affect us all in a negative or positive way. I hope this book will equip you with the simple tools required to accomplish your life goals. Equally, may you experience profound joy, great happiness, wisdom, insight, and lasting health.

It is not my intention to convert you toward or pull you away from any religion or your own beliefs, as that is your personal spiritual journey. For this reason I use the word universe, which is interchangeable. If you observe a faith, please let that faith guide you as you read the pages in this book and insert the word(s) God, Higher Power, Creator, or your sacred deity's name in the place of the word universe. If you are not religious, or if you do not believe in God, feel free to see the universe as the world you inhabit—all the beauty, power, and magnificence that surrounds you every day. The universe viewed either way offers a sea of limitless potential, especially when you believe it to be so.

May your love for yourself and your life deepen daily.

Introduction

If you are unhappy, frustrated, or disappointed by life, or if you are having trouble achieving your goals, this book is for you!

You create the circumstances in your life, sometimes on purpose and sometimes without your conscious knowledge. And everything in your life is constantly changing you, reprogramming you, making you the person you are today.

While the law of attraction is an unparalleled tool in achieving your goals, this rule forms only part of this strategy. I encourage you to go deeper by thinking about twelve specific areas in your life so you can know where to focus your attention, what to do, and what to avoid. When you recognize the blocks to your success and when you have the tools to overcome them, old limitations will no longer apply. Most importantly, your life will remain a mystery until you begin to hear life speaking to you!

Life Is Talking to You! *Are You Listening?*

Life whispers, but sometimes life screams at you. The next time you drop and smash a glass, notice "coincidences," or feel like everything is "all wrong," stop, think, listen, and decode these messages. When you understand how to interpret your everyday circumstances, your life will become easier and more predictable, fulfilling, and enjoyable.

Before I heard life talking to me, I struggled in every area of my life. The day I began to hear life was the day it all changed. From my darkest day in my most challenging year, the transformation of my marriage, career, finances, and life began. I had ignored all the warnings for the last time because I finally heard them. I wanted to avoid more painful lessons and I desperately wanted change. So I became a student of life; I started listening, researching, and learning.

I began by changing my previously unhappy marriage. By studying happy couples and reading many books on the mind and positive thinking, I created a simple formula so my husband and I could live as "honeymooners" again. When I wrote my first book, *Honeymooners Forever: Twelve-Step Marriage Survival Guide*, I was thrilled by the dramatic impact on my relationship, the relationships of my readers, and all the couples I was coaching! I was fascinated to see how this simple strategy often caused a snowball effect. The strategy instigated an attitude change, which created a positive energy change, which often ignited more dramatic "life changes" in the lives of the readers.

I studied and became a qualified relationship and crisis counsellor so I could help more people experience positive transformations in their relationships and lives. I spent the next few years reading books and learning more about psychology, counselling, the mind/body connection, alternative medicine, physics, hypnotherapy, paranormal events, and strategies for success. I compiled a strategy that simplifies the complicated.

I felt compelled to document my discoveries, observations, and strategies in this easy-to-understand book. I guide you through twelve important areas where life talks to us:

- ourselves
- thoughts

- emotions
- bodies
- instincts
- relationships
- love
- passions
- time
- money
- life's rules, and
- the universe

I explain, step by step, how to use many well-known psychological/counselling therapies as well as my newly created techniques so you may have increased focus and emotional strength, thereby reaching your potential.

This strategy has transformed my life, and I have witnessed amazing changes in the lives of many clients in my counselling practice. You can now use these same tools and experience the same success. Do the exercises and the homework, and be prepared to change. I wish you all the very best in life!

May you be astounded by the intricate and effortless ways in which *your* life speaks to you, assists you, warns you, and guides you while simultaneously loving and inspiring you.

Chapter Summary

Chapter 1 is all about you! I discuss your self-esteem, intuition, self-concept, inner child, and personality. I explore the real you versus the ideal you, increasing your personal power, coping with change, and describing ways you are influenced and changed by your environment without realizing. I help you discover your needs and wants, identify what separates you from (or unites you with) others, and I tell you why it is so vital to understand, accept, and love yourself.

Chapter 2 describes the influence of thought in your life. I show you how to monitor and change your thoughts or challenge unhelpful thoughts/beliefs using CBT (cognitive behaviour therapy). I outline the roles of the conscious and subconscious minds and then show you how to reprogram the subconscious mind. I shed light on the power of your words and attitudes. I show you how to change old self-sabotaging patterns of thoughts and behaviour, give you techniques for improving indecision, stressful days, or past trauma, and I explain the law of attraction and how to remain positive and improve upcoming events using your mind.

Chapter 3 explores your emotions. I give examples of how your emotions often warn you about issues in your current circumstances you may have overlooked, such as neglected needs. I give you proven psychological techniques to release trapped emotional pain from the past. I show you how to identify which areas of life are going well and which are not using "The Crisis Wheel," so you can make the required changes and move forward. I show you how to deal with anger, depression, fear, guilt, blame, and self-loathing, and I give you techniques to help you grieve and heal after a loss.

Chapter 4 explains how to listen to, respect, and love your body. I discuss the theories on avoiding sickness and disease and tell you how to increase your energy and avoid fatigue. Your body is always talking to you, whether it be a sore throat or chest infection. If negative thought patterns are contributing to your ill health, I will help you identify and change these. I discuss addictions and describe the dangers of alcohol abuse. I outline the benefits of rest, relaxation, and meditation.

Chapter 5 will help you understand your instincts. I write about pre-life purpose, creating heaven on earth, understanding your aura and chakras, and why life is like school. I outline the impact of different energies, including feng shui on your home and surroundings. I discuss miracles, blessings, screams from within (intuition warnings), how your brain accurately processes danger, the supernatural, and how to interpret your dreams and nightmares. I show you how to bring more peace into your life, increase your ability to concentrate, and help you focus in an emergency.

Chapter 6 will bring quality to your relationships. I discuss relationship therapy and family therapy, as well as give you lots of parenting tips to increase your child's self-esteem, while maintaining discipline. I discuss dysfunctional relationship patterns such as controlling spouses, codependency, and verbal or physical abuse cycles. I show you how to avoid an "energy vampire" or ways to become assertive and manage conflict better. I give you my new technique for instantly improving problematic relationships with workmates or relatives. I discuss why being a victim leaves you powerless and what creates, or breaks, this mentality.

Chapter 7 is the love and passions chapter. I show you how to increase the love in your life and outline reasons it's so vital to love your pets, home, workplace, and job or career. I ask you to find your passions and keep them alive, and why. I tell you why you most likely haven't achieved some goals, and then I give you my simple five-step technique for achieving goals and outlining what you need to do daily and monthly to stay on track. I discuss patience, perfectionism, and self-discipline. I give you exercises to stretch your mind so you can go beyond a limited mindset and begin to create with intention.

Chapter 8 focuses on time and money. In this chapter, I shed light on the mysterious way time seems to speed up and slow down, and why this happens. I show you how you can achieve more with less time, increase productivity, and increase the intensity and passion in your everyday experiences. I encourage you to examine your attitude toward money; by changing this relationship, you can easily change your financial status. Is your attitude toward money physical or spiritual? Use the chart to find out. I discuss fear of poverty, reducing debt, and how to be wealthy. Your financial freedom starts with your mind.

Chapter 9 outlines some of life's important rules. I encourage you to think about and follow these rules (and what may happen if you don't). I talk about predicting future events, how to be kind to your future self, and why you benefit by creating magical memories. I talk about blocks to success, how to overcome fear, stepping out of your comfort zone, and doing what you previously only dreamed of! When you follow the rules of life, you will increase the good energy, people, and experiences in your life and are likely to have less hectic or catastrophic experiences. I also show you how to learn about life by observing animals.

Chapter 10 discusses the many ways in which the universe is speaking to you by inspiring, helping, or warning you about dangers in your current path. I show you how to identify and interpret these messages. How do you know when it's time to change, go in a different direction, run, avoid an event, and more? I show you how. I also explain how to have confidence in your quick decisions, and why you must delay making others. I list well-known universal laws and talk about life's setbacks. Your life will become happier and easier, and you will achieve your goals much faster when you stop ignoring, and finally start hearing, life!

Most people spend their entire life imprisoned within the confines of their own thoughts. They never go beyond a narrow, mind-made personalized sense of self that is conditioned by the past.—Eckhart Tolle

You always behave consistently with the picture that you hold of yourself on the inside. Because of this, you can improve your performance by deliberately changing the mental pictures that you hold about yourself in that area.—Brian Tracy

Chapter 1

Are You Listening to Yourself?

You Are Special and Have a Purpose

You are perfection. You are a soul—a beautiful, loving soul that has come to this earth. You have been created in the miracle of conception. You are unique. You are here to make an impact. You are meant to be here, and there is no one in the entire universe exactly like you, not now or in the future. Your personality, childhood, experiences, goals, talents, and creative gifts, as well as your unique DNA, set you apart. No human is an accident, despite what some say. You are of great value to the human race and our universe. Your purpose is to be yourself, to be fulfilled and happy, and to live a life filled with love. You are blessed, and you will make a difference to this world. That is why you are here on earth.

You have a purpose in this life. It's your role to find that purpose. You will know when you are on track by the way you feel. If you feel unhappy, controlled, stressed, or miserable, then it's likely you have gotten a little off track.

You Have an Inbuilt Warning Device

You have an inbuilt warning device, an inner voice, a gut instinct, intuition, your higher self. Whatever you call it, this inner voice attempts to keep you on track with your inspirations and goals and helps motivate you toward achieving in life—or stops you on a destructive moment or life path. Your inner voice is normally soft and in the background. Yet if you are in a manipulative relationship or if you are not standing up for yourself, your inner voice becomes the voice inside screaming, *I've had enough! I don't want this anymore! I feel like I am being controlled. I need some peace! I don't want to be here right now. I want to get away. I'm sick of this. I can't take this anymore. I'm sick of doing everything for everyone else. I'm sick of myself.*

This inner voice is hugely powerful and important and should always be listened to. This inner voice is there to help you and can save your life or save you from a catastrophe. You may experience your inner voice as a hunch, an uneasy feeling, or something you can't explain, guiding your decision making. Some people choose to ignore this voice inside because they can logically argue the other position (the flipside) with alternative actions. Following your inner voice will usually lead to better decision making and a happier, more fulfilling life.

When you ignore your inner voice, you will become sick, stressed, and agitated more often. Once you learn to distinguish the difference between your thoughts and your inner voice, you can never mistake this wonderful presence again, and your life will improve dramatically. Allow your inner voice to make decisions for you, as this is your "gut instinct." Ideally, most of your activities would be based on how you "feel inside." Does it

4

feel right? Is it time to go? Do you feel you need a change? An inner voice often feels like a feeling rather than sounding like a voice. Ignoring your inner voice can be fatal to your happiness, and can put your life in danger, as this example illustrates:

Leanne's mother was very sick, dying from cancer, and Leanne would drive daily with her father to visit her mother in hospital. One day, for reasons Leanne could not explain, she told her father she could not come to the hospital that day. Leanne felt such a strong urge to stay home, and while she did not know why, it overpowered her. Her father was upset and annoyed, which made Leanne cry, but she knew there was a "reason" she had to stay home. On the way home from the hospital that day, her father was involved in a serious car accident through no fault of his own. His van was crushed beyond repair, except on the driver's side. He miraculously escaped serious injury. Yet if Leanne had been in the passenger seat, she would have been seriously injured or killed. Leanne listened to her inner voice, and it most likely saved her life!

Love and Accept Yourself

Love has the power to transform our lives and heal our bodies. Our journey of health, happiness, and success in life starts with two powerful words: self-love!

In my counselling room, many of the problems I see stem from a client's low self-love. Situations involving relationship struggles, depression, self-harm, codependency, indecision, controlling or abusive spousal patterns, jealousy, alcohol and drug addiction, and more are usually improved when a client's self-love increases. The healthier your self-love, the better your relationship with yourself, your partner, your children, and your world. Low self-love, often called low self-esteem, can be a result of neglect in childhood (where a child may not have received enough praise, support, and attention and instead may have received verbal or physical abuse from his or her parents).

Nonetheless, we can increase our self-esteem as an adult. We can make the positive changes right now. So if you are going through a hard time, look in the mirror and say, "I love you."

(If this is too hard, begin by saying, "I approve of you.") Do this as many times a day as you can, and then sit back and watch for the miracles. Start saying "I love you" throughout the day—you will find it amazing. All of a sudden you will care for yourself more, keep the house tidier, make more effort to keep up your appearance, and have more confidence in yourself and your choices. Stop criticizing yourself constantly like so many people do. It's such a beautiful thing to love and accept yourself, and when you do, it makes it so much easier for others to love and accept you. Love and accept the way you look—your body, your laugh, your unique sense of humour—love and cherish all that is you, and watch the miracles occur.

I first discovered this concept of self-love after reading *The Power Is within You* by Louise Hay, when I was in my twenties. I felt transformed through reading her book, and I have been a fan ever since. I finally had the honour of recently seeing her at a seminar in Melbourne, Australia. I spent weeks wondering what she might talk about, and I was so grateful to be able to hear her talk in person.

Louise experienced this power of self-love and acceptance through the healing of her own cancer, and she has been part of countless more healings worldwide. Louise's message was strong and powerful, like her books! It was all about the incredible power of self-love, affirmations, being mindful of our thoughts, our words, our self-talk, and doing mirror work and affirmations to improve our self-love.

Every word you say out loud, or in your mind, about yourself has a large impact on your self-esteem. We really need to listen to the words we use. We need to stop and analyze the way in which we talk about our self, and we need to ensure *all* our words are kind and loving. No longer say to yourself, "You idiot!" but instead say, "I tried and I will do better next time." Our world will change dramatically by simply changing our self-talk. Change right now and watch your life transform!

The Power of Your Self-Concept

We all have a self-concept, a self-ideal. Our self-concept affects the way in which we participate in the world. It is the pair of glasses through which we view our self and our experiences. Your self-concept is list of statements about yourself—a perception of who you are, what you do, and how you interact with others. Do you think you are overweight, fit, stupid, intelligent, lazy, highly motivated, funny, boring, outgoing, or shy? Make a list of all the things you believe you are. This is your self-concept (made popular by founder of person-centred therapy, Carl Rogers). This self-concept is your master program, and all your behaviours stem from this program. If you have a self-belief (self-concept) that you are awkward and you bump into someone you know in the supermarket, and this person says hi but then abruptly says, "I've gotta go," as a result of your negative self-concept, you may think, *Oh, I must have said something wrong. He thinks I'm an idiot. Of course he would try to avoid me.*

On the other hand, if your self-concept included positive thoughts like, *I am confident. I am fun. I am successful,* then you would most likely think positive thoughts: *He must be busy today. Oh well; I will catch up with him next time. I am in a bit of a rush anyway.* A poor self-concept, like poor self-esteem, can result from poor parenting, negative feedback you've received from your family and friends about yourself, or your experiences and negative self-talk. To improve your self-concept, you need to monitor your self-talk and do affirmations, which will be discussed at length in chapter 2.

You Have Needs

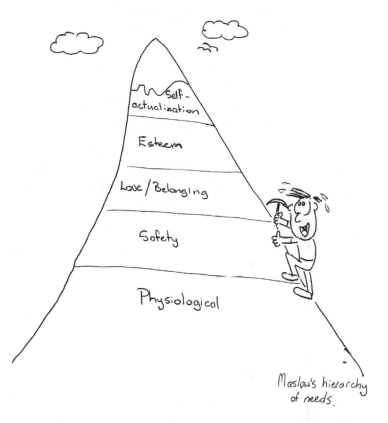

Maslow's hierarchy of needs.

Abraham Maslow's (1954) hierarchy of needs highlights the needs we must meet before moving forward. As we go through life, we all have needs/experiences at various stages in our lives that must be fulfilled. These include physiological needs, safety, love, belonging, esteem, and self-actualization. It is vital to be aware of your needs not just for yourself but for your family. It is helpful to keep these needs in mind as we ideally work through each stage toward self-actualization. We cannot meet needs on higher levels until they are met on lower levels. For example, if we are unhappy in life and lonely, we have a need in the "love and belonging" area, but we cannot fully focus on this if, for example, we do not have enough money for food or shelter. Finding accommodations should ultimately be our priority. So it's important to work through our needs in order.

You Are Everyone

Do you have a friend you tend to judge harshly? Have you asked yourself, *Why does she act like this? Why can't she get her sh*t together? Why doesn't she listen to me and heed my advice?* Is there someone you constantly think negatively about? Well, you are no different from the other person. The only thing that makes you different is what you have experienced. You are no different from anyone else on earth. If you had been through every experience they have, you would most likely act the same. So what makes you different? Experiences, and some genetic traits, differentiate you from your fellow human beings. If you had been born in their shoes, had grown up in their household, had the relationships they've had, lived in their culture, you would practically be them! At the very least you would behave like them. When you comprehend this, you can more readily accept and have empathy for others. It's vitally important to our lives, relationships, and our world to understand that we are all the same underneath. We all want to love, be loved, and be happy. We are just fortunate if we grew up without violence, poverty, victimization, verbal abuse, or cultural disharmony.

You Are Your Inner Child

From the time we are born, until approximately seven years of age, we readily accept most information without questioning it. We're a sponge for new information, but we do not have the mental capability or emotional maturity to filter out information that is not correct or helpful. We learn fast, and most of these thoughts, ideas, and impressions are stored in our subconscious and impact our behaviours and views as an adult. For example, if you witnessed a lot of fighting between your parents when you were six years old, in your adulthood you may believe high-conflict relationships are normal. So our inner child is greatly transformed by what we have witnessed as a child. According to psychologist and author B. F. Skinner, our behaviour changes in a series of stimulus/response reactions—life is cause and effect. We are not simply products of our environment; we are constantly changing our behaviours in relation to positive and negative reinforcements. Our habits, our reactions, and the way we behave are all learned as children and are in a state of constant fluctuation. Throughout life, we take with us our inner child and many of the behaviours, impressions, and beliefs from our childhood.

You Are Your Personality

Some people are naturally outgoing, others are naturally shy. Some are socially outgoing and some are reclusive, preferring their own company. According to Sigmund Freud, your personality is mostly established by the age of five. Whatever experiences occur throughout those early years impact and shape your personality in a fundamental way. Other theorists suggest you were born with your personality, that it is genetic and therefore hereditary. In contrast, behavioural theories support that an individual's behaviour is constantly shaped and changed by their environment. So from this viewpoint it would make sense that your personality changes and develops as you grow older. Regardless of how your personality originates and develops, you benefit greatly by accepting that *you are your personality*, so work with it, and embrace and love your personality.

We are generally more one extreme or the other of a personality trait. Some examples include:

- Dominant versus easygoing
- Extrovert versus introvert
- Friendly versus withdrawn
- Organized versus disorganized
- Spontaneous versus structured
- Leader versus follower
- Patient versus impatient
- Calm versus highly strung
- Creative versus practical

Know Yourself

Do you know who you are? Do you love being in the middle of conversations or prefer being on the sidelines? Do you like being direct and assertive with people, or do you hide your feelings? Are you rude or considerate, impatient or dramatic? Do you love to be with people, or are you withdrawn? Do you love talking about life's issues, such as relationships, sex, and spirituality—the deeper things? Or do you prefer to make lighthearted, general conversation? When you meet new people, do you dive headfirst into this new relationship, or do you put a wall up because you are shy or in case you get hurt? Do you really know yourself? Are you true to who you are?

Knowledge is power. Get to know yourself, accept yourself, and then do what makes you happy. As you take yourself everywhere you go, you need to keep yourself happy. If you know you are a social person, you will make yourself happy by including lots of social activities on your calendar. If you know you enjoy spending time alone, you may prefer to factor in lots of quiet time. Keep yourself happy by giving yourself what you need. To give yourself what you need, you need to know who you are and what you want.

Conflict Between the Real You and the Ideal You

The "real you" is the way you act, talk, and interact with yourself, others, and your world. The ideal you is the way you would like to be—the picture in your mind's eye about how you would like to think, react, feel, and behave. This ideal you may be based on a friend you know or a family member, or it may simply be an improved version of who you are or someone you aspire to be like. When the real you is very different from the ideal you, when you are not meeting the standards you consciously or subconsciously set for yourself, you will often experience emotional turmoil and feelings of restlessness, guilt, and frustration. Ultimately this can lead to maladjustment and unease.

What if the real you has trouble getting out of bed on time, has trouble cleaning up after yourself, or has little self-discipline and slips into some very self-destructive habits? Yet you, the same person, aspires to be hardworking, highly motivated, and career focused? The real you and the ideal you would be distant from each other. This will cause incongruity within yourself; your two selves will be out of alignment, and inner peace will remain elusive while you condemn yourself for constantly disappointing yourself.

Congruent—Be Yourself and Experience Profound Changes in Your Life

A counsellor and a client need to connect on an honest level for therapy to work well—and this is powerful! If a client senses a counsellor is not being genuine, he or she will emotionally pull away and close off. In counselling training, we are trained to be ourselves, or the client will not be. A counsellor cannot hide behind a mask, nor put on a false front; we need to meet the client as an equal.

Similarly in life, we can all experience deeper personal relationships by simply being ourselves, and we can do this all the time! No more fronts, no more holding back, no more brick walls, no more role-playing. We need to stop acting the way we think we should act, or how we think the other person expects us to act.

So how do we do this? We need to remove the ego. We need to become only spirit. We need to simply *be*. When we become more real, our life will become more real! This is the miracle of simply being ourselves—the spirit within, without the mask. The more real we are, the happier we are. For this reason, I ask my clients with depression this question: When in your life are you being the real you?

As we change, so will our life. If you are struggling just being yourself, try it out. When you meet people, be 100 percent congruent. It's such an exciting and freeing feeling, and of course it takes a conscious effort to do this. When you meet someone and are 100 percent genuine, he or she usually responds to you in the same honest, congruent, and sincere way. You will find that your relationships strengthen faster, and you will connect on a deeper, more intimate level with everyone. You will genuinely get to know people and gain more friends. Your interactions and your life will become more wonderful and fulfilling as you become authentically real.

In childhood, we learn from others. In our teenage years, we copy others. In adulthood, our biggest rewards come from simply *being* ourselves.

Self-Actualization Is a Place of Peace

When your real self and your ideal self are aligned (congruent) and as one, when the standards you set for yourself in your life, activities, and relationships are consistent with the best version of yourself, then you are thought to experience everything and everyone as your *unique self.* Through this interaction, where you are totally present and consistently the best version of yourself, you are said to have reached *self-actualization.* Self-actualization is very much a part of some counselling therapies, mainly person-centred therapy, which was founded by psychologist Carl Rogers. Some people become self-actualized in their twenties, others in their forties, and others never. When you are self-actualized, you are living in harmony with who you want to be. Once you are self-actualized, the old limitations no longer apply. You are only limited by your imagination. You flow with the process of life and experience greater success and joy.

Who Do You Think You Are?

You may be someone's child, brother, or sister, an employee, employer, or a student. You may be a footballer, a dancer, housewife, father, mother, or scholar. You have so many roles, so many hats to put on, and these roles may confuse you, leaving you feeling lost. So what are you for sure? You are a body, you are a soul, you are a mind ... and these three things together make you. You are your parents, your culture, your school or workmates, your society, your country. These factors all influence your choices in life and all contribute to who you are, and, importantly, they contribute to your personal power. I believe we are all fingers of the same glove, the shared glove of humanity. We are all capable of great power and creating miracles. Be constantly on the lookout for the miracles in your personal and professional life. Accept this power and gratefully accept these blessings. It's thrilling to be part of our beautiful cosmos. I believe there is a spirit in every human, animal, and plant—in every part of our universe. You are incredibly powerful, beyond your wildest imagination! Accept your vital role, and use this power for the good of yourself and our world.

The World Revolves around *You*!

When I was a self-centred teen, and my dad was having trouble coping with my egocentric ways, he would become frustrated and say, "The world doesn't revolve around you!" Well, many years later, I realized he was wrong because the world does revolve around me. It revolves around him and it revolves around every person on earth. We can only experience life from this perspective—from being the centre of our own world. It is impossible to experience our life any other way. You are in control of your own mini universe—your own world. When you walk down the road, you may be thinking about your life, relationships, situations, and appointments, and the person who just walked past you is thinking about his life, relationships, situations, and appointments. Funny, isn't it? Everyone is living in the centre of his and her own universe.

So if you're not happy with your life, take the reins! You have the power. And with the tools in this book, you can make the difference and become the power centre of *your* much-improved universe.

You Have Power

We have power and choices. Sometimes we may think life is "all charted out." Yet at any point in time, there is nothing (physically) stopping us from doing some ridiculous things. You could jump up right now, wherever you are, and sing out loud, "I've got the power!" while simultaneously clapping, stomping your feet, and smiling. We have the power to do silly things, intelligent things, dangerous things, mundane things … but most of all, we have the power to improve our lives. We have the power to control ourselves and our impulses or to manipulate others. We have the power to deeply love our families and ourselves. We have the power to love our children, friends, strangers, teachers, workmates, and even our bosses! We have the power to affect others—to make or break their day. We can help strangers and we can help friends. We can make an impact on other people's worlds in a negative or loving way.

What would you want to do in life if you acknowledged your power, combined with the 100 percent belief that you would succeed? Just think about that.

You Never Stay the Same

Stop for a moment and make a mental list of the people you admire. These could be celebrities, sports people, friends, neighbours, family, etc. We admire different people for their different strengths. By admiring people, by looking and saying, "Wow, that's what I want. I wish I could be more like that," we begin to change. We are always evolving, and if we are focused, we will continue to improve the way we live, interact with others, handle money, view our lives, and improve who we are.

We evolve by learning from those we admire. We can learn so much from people we admire. We can become better parents, partners, business owners, or employees. We can learn to manage our time more effectively. We can become fitter and healthier. Every day, we are changing. By accepting this constant change, in ourselves and others, we will experience more peace. In my counselling practice, my role involves helping individuals and couples to accept change.

Nature teaches us how to cope with change. Tree branches move with the wind and cope with storms, and most are flexible enough to resist changes in the environment. Most branches bend with the wind, but the branch that tries to resist will break, just as the person resistant to change will become angry and tense. You can create a new you anytime you want. You can fail high school and still go on to run a million-dollar company when you are an adult. The exciting thing about change is *change begets change.* When you change (and improve) in one area of your life, it will affect other areas of your life, like a snowball or domino effect. How? Well, if you are strong enough to give up smoking, then you are most likely going to feel more confident when tackling other poor habits. If you become more assertive through a workplace training program, you can use this assertiveness in your everyday life and improve in other areas too. The faster you make positive changes, the faster your world will be transformed, like a ripple effect. There are no limits, except the ones you impose on yourself.

You Are What You Watch on TV

We are influenced by our family, the people we associate with, and our co-workers, but seldom do we think about how greatly we are influenced by watching television—and the ramifications for our life.

Diane's relationship was a constant challenge. One of her main issues was jealousy. She seemed overly suspicious of her husband's behaviour, terrified he would have an affair. While there was no evidence of this, she would begin to worry if he was late home from work, and watch him closely on the computer. She felt overly concerned about his relationships with his female workmates. She even hired a detective once to check up on him. I asked Diane to look at this issue a little deeper. Where was her excessive fear coming from? Was it due to a past relationship, any affairs she may have had, or her childhood? Diane laughed as she told me of a TV show she was "hooked on," where the couples all sleep around behind each other's backs. This seemed to be the only link, so I asked Diane to stop watching the show for a month to see if her jealousy improved. Diane stopped watching this TV show, her favourite at the time, and her suspicions were reduced rapidly, and her relationship improved just as fast!

Diane's relationship was being harmed by her TV watching, as week after week her belief that married men cheat was being reinforced in her subconscious. And as we act and think in accordance with our subconscious thoughts, Dianne was reacting to fears in her subconscious based not on reality but on an imaginary TV world.

Which television shows do you regularly watch? Are they positive and uplifting? They are becoming part of who you are, so be careful what you put into your brain and what filters through to your subconscious. As our actions, feelings, and thoughts are influenced greatly by our subconscious, we need to be careful about the messages we let in. Watching television can really detrimentally affect our lives. Try going without the news or muting the advertisements. Be particular about which shows you choose to watch and see if this has a positive effect on your life. We are all sponges; we are all soaking up our environments, becoming part of them, being transformed by them, whether we like it or not.

Remember, not all stories are told through the media or on TV. There are millions of positive messages and miracles, stories of love and empowerment that do not make it to the daily news.

You Are Not Your Past

Your past is only a memory and a learning tool. Don't let the past hold you back; it doesn't need to be part of you if you don't want it to be. Keep what you like and let the rest go. Every day your body is renewing itself, and your cells are constantly being replaced. You can replace a negative version of yourself, transform yourself into a new you, any time at all. And even if other people label you, you are exactly what *you* think you are. Many people are prisoners of their past; they let it hold them back. They don't believe in the power of letting go. That doesn't work for me!

Let's assume you lacked confidence and felt like a loser at school as a teenager, like I did. I felt awkward, not part of the "in crowd." I had pale legs, frizzy hair, and an uncontrollable fringe. I felt unattractive and wanted to sink through the concrete and become invisible when cute boys at school walked past. I was not in the popular group; I was an outsider.

But I do not let my experience in school hold me back. I created a new me. I was too scared to sing in front of the class, yet as a young adult I became a professional singer. I was terrified of public speaking, and now I speak publicly with confidence. I felt like life was limited, but now I believe in a world with no limitations. Would you like to join me? Would you like to create a new, improved version of yourself? You are limited only by your imagination—not your past! Join me in creating a new you—it is so much fun.

Homework—Are You Listening to Yourself?

1. List the times in your life when you have felt or heard a warning from within from your gut instinct/intuition about an upcoming event or a person you have met.
2. Test yourself: Why is having healthy self-esteem so important?
3. How do you see yourself? List your good and bad points, your likes and dislikes.
4. List your personality traits (e.g., are you mostly outgoing or shy, fearful or confident?). If you are unsure, ask your friends and family for input.
5. List everything about yourself in terms of the "real you" versus the "ideal you."
6. When are you the "real" you? Who in your life sees the real you?

The average person has seventy thousand thoughts per day.—Laboratory of Neuro Imaging, UCLA School of Medicine, Los Angeles, California. (http://www.loni.ucla.edu/About_Loni/education/brain_trivia.shtml)

All thoughts congeal; all thoughts meet other thoughts, criss-crossing in an incredible maze of energy, forming an ever-changing pattern of unspeakable beauty and unbelievable complexity.—Neal Donald Walsch

CHAPTER 2

ARE YOU LISTENING TO YOUR THOUGHTS?

Change Your Thoughts—Change Your Life

Our thoughts are the most important tool we have for improving our lives. Our thoughts create our reality—so when we change our thoughts, our reality will change. Everything we do and experience involves or starts with our thoughts. If we are unhappy with an area of our lives, first we need to think about what is not working and then think about the changes required, and focus on positive thoughts and action, surrounding the changes we seek. Our thoughts create the world we live in.

What are your thoughts about your life, body, relationships, family, work, neighbourhood, and the world you inhabit? You have choices about how you feel in these areas and how you run your life. In a split second you can change the energy around these areas from negative to positive, simply with your thoughts. You have the power.

What are you saying to yourself all day, every day? What have you said to yourself about your future, past, and present? Your thoughts are the central part of your achievements. If you are not receiving enough from life, think more deeply; think outside the box, and ultimately, think more positively. What do you want? Be precise. Create your ideal present and future by controlling your thoughts. We are always thinking, keeping our thoughts focused on what we want, not what we don't want. Our lives are moved in the direction of our dominant thoughts. It is not rocket science. What we focus on will manifest in our lives. If you want a life filled with peace, joy, success, abundance, love, fun, and friends, try to keep your mind firmly focused on these areas. It's your mind, so take charge. When you control your mind, you control most of your life.

Who Is inside Your Head?

We have a voice inside our head. Sometimes this voice works for us and sometimes it works against us. It is a combination of many influences you have experienced since you were a child: parents, teachers, and people of authority. You may feel as though your mother, father, grandparents, siblings, teachers and even influences from the media are all residing in your head—because they are! Up until eighteen years of age, these authority figures come in handy and can be lifesaving, but are they still needed? Don't you want to have your own opinions? Do you seek independence? Are you creating your own path? These voices are distracting and can hold you back. That is why you need to monitor these thoughts!

Are these some of the negative messages you say to yourself? "I am useless. I am fat. I am never going to get anywhere. I will always be alone. I can't make a decision. I can't control myself. I am getting old. I have no friends. My life sucks. Life is so hard. I can't seem to stay in relationships. No one will hire me. I am lazy. My life is pointless." In counselling, these thoughts that seem to pop into our minds randomly are called automatic thoughts.

To stop negative, repetitive, and dysfunctional thoughts, you may find it helpful to use any of the following two techniques:

1. Thought stopping using a rubber band, from RET (rational emotive therapy), developed by psychologist Albert Ellis.

   - Place a rubber band on your wrist and flick it when you hear these negative thoughts.
   - Be more aware of your language and remove "I should" from your self-talk.
   - Challenge these thoughts. How realistic are they?

2. The ABC model from CBT (cognitive behaviour therapy), developed by psychiatrist Aaron Beck. Cognitive behavior therapy assists with many irrational thoughts, such as overgeneralizations, self-deceptions, incorrect judgments, black and white thinking, all-or-nothing thinking, focusing only on the negative, perfectionism, jumping to conclusions, and more.

The ABC model (cognitive behaviour therapy) assists by looking at events versus reaction. When you experience an unsettling event, you can easily use this model. When you recognize self-defeating or irrational thoughts, you can replace them with positive ones, making the experience less stressful.

A. Activating event: seeing a friend down the street who ignores you.
B. Belief: you believe the friend saw you and turned away, so she must not like you.

C. Consequence emotionally: you feel sad, think you are not worthy of friends and that no one likes you.

By challenging and changing B (your belief, which is your automatic thoughts), you can change C (your emotional consequence). For example, if you changed B to thinking, *Maybe my friend was just busy, or didn't see me,* you would avoid all the negative emotions in C.

This ABC model is often used by doctors, psychiatrists, psychologists, and counsellors who work with clients, to assist them to self-monitor and change self-defeating thought patterns. If, after doing these techniques, you are still overwhelmed by negative thoughts, please seek help from a counsellor, psychologist or doctor.

Monitor Your Thoughts

Have you ever noticed when you are walking the dog, driving the car, or sitting on the bus the thoughts that seem to flow through your mind like waves? *I must get this done. I must do that. I look terrible today. I'll never pass that test.*

We need to ensure this self-talk is kind and productive. These thoughts can be negative, nasty, and unreasonable. If negative, self-talk can cause deep sadness and make us ill.

Despite the number of books I have read over the past twenty years on the power of the mind, I had my biggest breakthrough only a few years ago, reading *The Power of Now* by Eckhart Tolle. Eckhart discusses the concept that most of what goes through our mind is very repetitive and that we need to monitor this mind of ours. Stop taking as gospel the thoughts that run through your mind. We need to stop and question our thoughts. Is this correct? Is this true? Sometimes we simply need to write our thoughts down and analyze them. Sometimes we need to discuss and test them. Are they correct? Are they wrong? Use a diary to record your thoughts, especially when you are emotional.

Think It, Taste It, Receive It

Taste success before it happens. This is an integral part of goal setting, and it is powerful!

Recently I was talking with a man who was starting a new business venture, working for himself. I asked him, "Do you have a business plan? Do you have an idea of where you want this business to take you?" He said yes. He explained that he had a business degree and could see exactly what he wanted to achieve, and while he lacked some confidence, it seemed very straightforward. He had it all planned.

When I asked him, "Can you taste it?," he looked at me with surprise. He didn't understand what I was asking.

Can you taste success? Can you taste what it feels like to receive the rewards you seek? Can you feel it?

I explained that our minds and what we put "out there" is powerful, but a thought without emotion is like a match without a spark. It is not enough to think, *I want to be a success. I want a successful career, a sports car, a pool, a mansion, a wonderful, passionate relationship.* We need to see ourselves in this picture, feel what it *feels* like ... *taste* it, as if we have these items and this relationship already, as if the success has already been achieved. Feel how it would *feel* to achieve your goal, such as to be a successful business owner, debt free, happily married, or happily single. If you have no *emotion*, there will be limited *motion*, so taste success before you try to achieve it.

The Thought Process

What is thought? First of all, thought can be divided into two areas—conscious and subconscious thought.

Conscious Thought is what you normally think about at any given point. Regardless of how intricate our thought process is, we are only able to hold one thought at a time in our conscious mind. Things such as, "I must remember to put the washing away." The conscious mind is responsible for all your voluntary physical actions. It is the part of the brain responsible for logic and reason. The conscious mind has trouble recalling everything perfectly. It filters the information that goes in and out of the subconscious. It acts like a gatekeeper.

The Subconscious Mind: While the subconscious performs many tasks, the following nine are vital:

1. *Storage Device:* The subconscious acts like a huge warehouse for all your thoughts, beliefs, and memories of everything you have ever seen and experienced, as well as your attitudes, fears, and some ideas you are usually not aware of. The subconscious also stores all the information for your programmed activities and skills (such as walking, driving a car, playing a sport, etc.).

2. *Initiates Emotions and Thoughts:* While emotions are often directly related to your thoughts, you can have emotional reactions that are knee-jerk reactions to your subconscious feelings, ideas, and attitudes. Your automatic thoughts (the thoughts that just pop into your minds as if from nowhere) are usually triggered by your core values, beliefs, and ideas, which are all stored in your subconscious. So in many cases, our subconscious triggers our emotions and thoughts.

3. *Influences Speech:* When you communicate with others, much of your conversation stems from the subconscious, as it stores your belief system, your self-concept, your ideas about life, and your attitudes. Moreover, in Freudian psychoanalysis, your subconscious thoughts/feelings can come through as a slip of a tongue, called a "Freudian slip." You may say what you are thinking, what you may not be consciously aware of, *not* what you were planning to say.

4. *Affects Your Behaviour:* So this incredible computer, the subconscious, is responsible for your knee-jerk reactions in life, love, business, relationships, and more. Your subconscious propels you through life, directing you. It is the master program that many of your actions, emotions, reactions to others, and attitude to life originate from. If we can change these internal beliefs and programs, we can change our life! (I will show you how to instigate this powerful change later in this chapter.)

5. *Defence Mechanism:* Our subconscious will often suppress painful memories. According to Sigmund Freud, your subconscious mind stores your repressed memories, which may be traumatic; these may slip through to a person's consciousness in dreams. In many situations, suppressed (hidden) traumatic memories can cause dysfunctional behaviour, or in some extreme cases, psychosis.

6. *Fast and Powerful:* The subconscious mind is many times faster than the conscious mind, and much more powerful. Think about how fast you react to near misses while driving. Before you have time to analyze the car that has just pulled out in front of you, your foot hits the brake, you move to a different part of the road, and your heart is pounding. These fast reactions are controlled by this incredibly fast computer— the subconscious.

7. *Finds Answers and Problem Solves:* The subconscious mind is like your own personal secretary—except it never sleeps! You may be thinking, *Oh, I forgot that person's name,* and then remember it hours later. While your conscious mind is on other things like watching TV, resting, and socializing, your subconscious mind is actively problem solving.

8. *Keeps You Alive:* The subconscious mind is responsible for keeping you alive, coordinating all your organs in perfect harmony. The subconscious is responsible for keeping your heart beating, your lungs continually functioning, and your central nervous system working, and it coordinates all the billions of your cells, day after day, year after year, until you die.

9. *Likes Consistency:* The subconscious keeps you behaving, speaking, and functioning in accordance with the standards set in your subconscious mind. This is why change is so incredibly hard. Your subconscious mind is king of

homeostasis—it keeps everything in your body functioning well, day after day, year after year, and it is not a fan of change. Your subconscious mind wants to keep you in your comfort zone. Your subconscious mind loves routine. How else could it coordinate your organs so perfectly? This is why when you want to change it is difficult—but not impossible! I will show you how.

Reprogram Your Mind

The subconscious mind is the warehouse of information, but this storage system controls much of your behaviour. This mass of information creates many of your emotions, impacts your behaviour, changes the way you view and perform in life, hides things from you, and keeps you functioning the same way you always have.

So how do you change? Well, your subconscious does not reason—the conscious mind does. Your subconscious accepts new programs, as long as the program passes through the gatekeeper. The conscious mind is the gatekeeper. If you convince your conscious mind of a new plan, idea, or self-concept, it will filter through to your subconscious mind. If you can change your thoughts in the conscious, the subconscious will obey the commands from the conscious mind. The conscious mind needs to accept this new information and filter it. Let's assume you want to change an unhelpful habit. First you will need to reprogram your thoughts if you wish to improve your life.

More than ten years ago I tried to give up smoking cigarettes. I tried more than twenty times. Then I listened to *Passion, Profit & Power* by Marshall Sylver, one of my favourite authors. One tape was designed for giving up smoking, and Marshall spoke of becoming excited about being a non-smoker, about admiring non-smokers, watching what they do with their hands, how they cope without cigarette smoking. This tape was integral to my success, and I was able to become excited about being a non-smoker and called myself a non-smoker even before I was! Marshall Sylver is a world-renowned hypnotist. He is experienced in retraining the subconscious, which is an integral part of changing our habits.

Habits are very difficult to change. Why? Because our subconscious mind is so powerful! It has been said that our thoughts are only up to 10 percent conscious and up to 90 percent subconscious. This explains why we try to change yet have great difficulty, as our subconscious mind may have many thoughts and provide reasons why we do not want to change the habit. Being aware of many of these "hidden thoughts" and working with our "hidden motivations" can help us achieve the changes we seek, not to mention working on retraining our conscious and subconscious minds. We need to ensure our mindset is right before we take the first step toward change. We are constantly programming our thoughts, so we need to consciously decide what we want and then carefully reconstruct our thoughts and words. After our thoughts, words, and emotions are in alignment, action can begin.

Once I changed my conscious thoughts and convinced that part of the mind, the message made it through to my subconscious. I changed my thoughts, feelings, and beliefs around smoking and smokers. Once I admired non-smokers, used positive self-talk, called myself a non-smoker, and became excited about success, I was ready for action! I have never turned back (or lit up another cigarette). By convincing my conscious mind, my subconscious mind followed and I became a non-smoker.

Positive Affirmations Will Transform Your Mind

When we use positive affirmations correctly, our lives can change, fast! A positive affirmation is a personalized statement that we create (on purpose) and then repeat out loud to ourselves, often. It must relate to the present moment, and be believable, for our subconscious to change. The aim of affirmations is to make positive changes in areas of our lives, such as: relationships, self-esteem, career, health, finances, habits and more. When we use affirmations correctly, we change the master programs in our subconscious, such as programs for how we view our self and our lives, how we behave and interact with others, what we expect, and much more. The subconscious mind can easily become full of negative thoughts (weeds), as our subconscious mind is always being changed by default. I view affirmations as the flowers we plant in our conscious minds, which filter through to the subconscious and create magical, positive, and lasting change. We ultimately want our entire mind to be a fertile ground for positive thoughts, and when we use affirmations, we compensate for negative thoughts. We also build on the positive. A strong, positive frame of mind equals a strong, positive life. Affirmations are something we can control, and we can use affirmations when we see a need. I work with affirmations; they are incredibly powerful, as they help change the negativity surrounding various areas. I also encourage most of my clients to use affirmations.

Here is an affirmation exercise to try. If you are feeling sad, depressed, stressed, indecisive, etc., think for a few minutes and then pick five areas in which your life has become difficult and could do with improvement. Write these five areas down and then create an affirmation for each. It is necessary that you create affirmations that feel believable, as your conscious mind needs to accept these new ideas before they can be accepted by the subconscious mind. (Remember, the conscious mind is like a gatekeeper.)

Your list could look like this:

Areas that need improving	Affirmation
I have no confidence.	I love myself (I approve of myself).
I'm sick of work; all I seem to do is work.	I love life and life loves me back.
I have no friends and most people don't like me.	I make friends easily. I am lovable.
I feel so worried and stressed about the future.	I am safe. I trust the process of life.
I don't like confrontation; others walk all over me.	I stand up for myself. I am powerful.
I can't stop thinking about my ex-partner.	It's my life and I make myself happy.

If you do not *love* your life, work on making it more exciting and fulfilling. Think about what is not working for you and instigate change. Have the expectation that *if you love your life— your life will love you back!* (I love this affirmation.) Maybe you could print out some great affirmations, keep them handy, and read them many times during the day.

Be Careful What You Wish For!

Our bodies are always listening to our minds, and accordingly, when we want something, our bodies and our environment may assist. How? Well, we continually send out energy, thoughts, and feelings into the world, and they are often enough to change upcoming events. If we are unsatisfied with our work, friends, or partner, this negative energy is with us everywhere. Sometimes it's so strong it may seem the universe is conspiring to help us have what we want. The universe can help us (or hinder us) in any number of ways, such as losing car keys, traffic jams, unexpected delays, sickness, additional time-consuming tasks needing to be done urgently, job losses or job opportunities, friends dropping in, friends cancelling plans, flights being delayed, extra bills arriving, work increasing, children becoming ill, and much more.

Has this ever happened to you? Have you not wanted to go somewhere and then became ill so you didn't (or couldn't) go? Or what about the time you were dreading an upcoming event and then you lost the car keys, and when you finally found them it was too late to make it? (You did not want to go anyway, so the universe helped.) What if you were unhappy at work and your poor energy, your lack of enthusiasm (not based on your words or work performance, but the unseen energy, the unspoken attitude), influenced the manager's decision to retrench you in the latest cutbacks? (You were somehow pleased, as you wanted to work elsewhere, but lacked the courage to make a change.) How many times have you heard about someone's spouse simply up and leaving his partner of twenty years, without any warning? Was it possible the deserted spouse was secretly wishing the relationship would end in some small part of her mind? Is it possible this negative energy motivated the spouse to leave? Could she have been "secretly" sabotaging the relationship and avoiding the spouse, hoping he would leave?

Nothing is a *secret* to the universe. What we don't say yet think in our private thoughts, and what we feel strongly about influences people—and it influences the world around us! The universe is listening and responding to our conscious and subconscious thoughts, the thoughts we talk about and the thoughts we keep hidden. *The universe sees and hears all.* We impact our future with *every* thought, so we need to censor our thoughts and ensure they are in our best interest. What we focus on expands. What we want often happens. I believe strongly that the universe is like our bottle with a genie in it, and our thoughts, verbalized or not, are our commands. So we need to be careful. I have experienced this power of the mind and since then have been very careful about what I wish for.

One dramatic example happened many years ago. I was just about twelve weeks pregnant, tired and running late for work. All I wanted was a day off. I felt like just calling the boss and saying I was sick, but my boss was really strict, so I didn't. I was really looking forward to my new life as a new mum, and work just didn't seem that important to me anymore. But still I got ready, begrudgingly, and started to drive to work. I kept thinking, over and over, *I don't want to go to work. I want a day off!* I was halfway to work and approaching a large intersection when I took my eyes off the road for a moment. When I looked back, the car in front of me had remained stationary even though the lights had changed to green. I was probably driving at about sixty kilometres an hour, the roads were wet, and I had nowhere to go and no time for fancy manoeuvres. I slammed on the brakes and prepared for the impact. I skidded, as if in slow motion, and could not avoid slamming into the back of the car. I suffered whiplash and was traumatized, and both cars were very badly damaged, but I did get my day off work. I spent it on the couch, taking Rescue Remedy (a wonderful remedy in cases of stress and trauma), and trying to rest to avoid a miscarriage. And while the sound of the crash and the feeling of the impact kept reverberating through my consciousness all day, I told myself I had learnt a very important lesson—if we want something bad enough, the universe will often conspire to make it happen, so we need to be careful what we wish for.

Sleep on Big Decisions

The mind is far more powerful than we give it credit. Have you ever heard the old saying "Sleep on big decisions"? Well, it works! It's amazing how you can make a decision and be absolutely 100 percent positive you've made the right choice, and then wake up the next day and say, "What was I thinking?" and re-evaluate your decision. Many times we can benefit by listening to our wise subconscious mind, which seems to do all the reasoning and calculating even while we sleep.

While we are sleeping, our subconscious mind is able to process the information at hand, weigh the pros and cons and our options, and bring intuition into the decision-making process. By involving this intuition, we often awake with a "gut-feeling" answer. Ultimately, sleeping on decisions is a great way to really "feel" what is right or wrong for us. Sometimes we still don't have an answer, other times we wake with full confidence about which direction to take. The subconscious mind is a crucial tool to use when faced with big decisions, so hand over your options to your subconscious, sleep soundly, and wait to make a decision when it feels absolutely right.

You Are a Magnet

Some years ago, one of my good friends had become deeply saddened due to a difficult break-up. She had become really negative, which affected all areas of her life for some time. I tried to help her understand that regardless of how her life seemed to be turning out, she needed to keep her mind focused on the positives. She was focused on being alone, angry toward the "other woman," and frustrated by her life, and she kept complaining about how powerless she felt. She was filled with anger, disappointment, hurt, and self-pity, and she felt like a victim. It's natural to feel this way after a break-up, and while we need time to mourn our losses, I felt my friend was spiralling out of control on a spiritual level.

Her life was the law of attraction in action. Because she was continually thinking negative thoughts, she kept attracting more negative experiences, which added to her negative thoughts and expectations. While my friend continued to feel like a victim, that life was unkind, cruel, and that she had no control, her reality would reflect just that! Her opportunities for healing, happiness, peace, and a new relationship were small while her thoughts remained negative. I encouraged her to be grateful for her children, secure job, and the roof over her head and focus on the many positives in her life. I was desperate to help her understand the importance of changing her thoughts.

Then I had an idea. I saw in my mind's eye a liquorice allsorts lolly. I told her that life is like a liquorice allsorts, and that she needs to stay in the pink and white (the positive thoughts), and avoid the black (the negative thoughts) if she wanted her life to improve. My friend understood this simple analogy and worked on changing her focus to more positive thoughts.

We humans naturally attract what we focus on, and when we focus on the negative, our energy changes, affecting our environments and relationships. People are either repelled by us, want to argue with us, or bombard us with their complaints about life. When we feel angry, flustered, impatient, and resentful, we are more likely to drop dishes, have car accidents, and miss the beauty in our lives. While we cannot see how the universe works, we know everything is simply atoms, and atoms are made up of energy, so the whole universe is simply energy. When we radiate negative energy, we become a magnet for negative experiences, conditions, people, and relationships. When we radiate positive energy, we become a magnet for positive experiences, conditions, people, and relationships.

The law of attraction suggests that we attract into our life circumstances, people, and conditions that relate to our strong and repetitive thoughts and beliefs, whether they are conscious or subconscious. When we walk through life with positive expectation and energy, we experience life's sunshine most of the time. Yet when we walk through life with negative expectation and energy, we may feel as though the storm comes just to rain on us.

Feed Your Soul

We are a blank canvas and often listen to the radio, watch television, and read newspapers, filling ourselves with many negative messages. We invest time learning how to improve our bodies, our health, and our money, yet many of us forget about our minds. We cannot possibly filter out *all* the negative messages that impact our subconscious—messages of lack, powerlessness, fear, anger, violence, famine, suffering, war, and destruction. While we can try to avoid the media, we can also be proactive by feeding our brains (and souls) with positive messages to keep our souls in balance.

We can listen to positive-thinking, self-help CDs. We can read books, like this one, on how to improve our lives. We are always growing, so we benefit by continually feeding our souls with positive messages—messages of hope, love, power, possibilities, miracles, abundance, pleasure, joy, and faith. To be positive we need to keep our minds positive, and sometimes this may seem a little too challenging in our current day and age. Keep your mind positive and strong by continually feeding it with positive messages.

Positive Projection—Mentally Rehearse Future Events

When you think positively about a future event and run through it through your mind as turning out perfectly, you will have a far greater chance of a more-positive experience. I used my "positive projection" technique for my first major television appearance back in 2007.

When the assistant from a TV network called my office asking if I would like to be on a popular morning show the next week, I instantly said yes. I started my positive thinking that moment and I kept it up all week. I imagined myself and Susie, the host, sitting together having a lovely, friendly chat. My goal was to relax and be myself during the interview. I never, not for a second, let myself entertain any negative thoughts ... *not one*. I would not let any friends or family even discuss any possible ways I may "stuff up." I needed the energy around the interview to be pure and positive. My mind was like a rock.

I kept visualizing, over and over (countless times!) myself and the host, sitting relaxed ... just chatting. The interview lasted five minutes exactly, and by the time I was ready for my first sip of water, it was all over. That night, celebrating over a glass of champagne, I was on a natural high; I knew this day and this feeling was one I would savour for years to come. I had just appeared on national TV and been interviewed about my first book, *Honeymooners Forever*. I had been calm, collected, and looked professional. I attribute my sense of calm to the positive projections that I practiced all week prior to the interview.

You can use positive projection for job interviews, holidays, goals, first dates, projects, and examinations—anything important in your life. Positive projection works. You are creating a new, positive future with your mind, emotions, and energy.

Negative versus Positive Thoughts

Our desires are achievable; however, we need to be spiritually open and not focused on negatives, as that negative energy will work against us in the fulfilment of our desires. We need to be a ball of love, a ball of pure and positive spirit to attract more blessings and to increase the chances for our goals to materialize. So how do we do this? Well, I just recently discovered the secret and am thrilled to share it with you.

Many years ago, when I wrote my first book, I would wait for inspiration. Once inspired I would start to write. I waited for moments to "come over me" before I could write more pages. I have since discovered that creativity is available to us all *at any time*. But we need to do one thing in order to be creative. We need to feel at one with our world and at peace.

We need to become a channel of pure light, just spirit. To do this, we need to release all negative thoughts and emotions. We need to live in this moment. Sure, we are earthbound humans and not perfect. We get angry, we have grievances, and we become emotionally distracted. Yet if we want to feel free, pure love in a state of acceptance at one with our world, we benefit by not hanging on to the negative emotions. We must work through these negative emotions as quickly as possible, so we can go back to peace. Obviously if we are grieving over a loss, such as the loss of a loved one, this takes longer, and then time helps us heal. Nonetheless, with grievances and hurts, we are ideally aiming to resolve these issues and get back to feeling positive emotions as soon as possible.

To resolve our resentments with others, we need to talk to the people involved, write letters, diarize, seek counselling, or do whatever it takes to be in balance again. We need to remove those negative emotions from our energy. When we accept our self, our family, our friends, and our humanity, we can become a channel of love, filled with creativity—our souls seem open to the heavens. When we are filled with negative thoughts, we feel angry, frustrated, rushed, annoyed, or bitter, and our creativity, our concentration, and our ability to make a positive impact is hindered. We have temporarily slowed down the flow of love from ourselves to the world and back.

To increase our flow of love, we need to forgive, accept others without judgment, and love ourselves, our life, and others. When our minds focus on positive thoughts, our creativity increases, people seem to be lovingly drawn to us, and we experience less conflict. We are more likely to experience continual peace and joy.

When our minds are stuck on negative thoughts, we experience more conflict and struggle and less peace. We become spiritually imbalanced and lose our peace when we are focused on negative thoughts. If you find yourself focused on negative thoughts, acknowledging this is half the battle.

Once we admit this and then work on forgiveness, showing empathy, understanding and releasing blame (whatever we need to process to work through our emotions) to enable us to reach a state of peace and focus once again on positive thoughts, we regain our power. We just need to honestly admit when we are focused on unhelpful, negative thoughts and move to positive thoughts. You may have unresolved issues keeping your thoughts focused on the negative, and you may need additional help from a counsellor or psychologist. Our natural and most enjoyable state is one of peace, joy, and love.

If we operate mostly from the ego, we are more likely to feel distant from others, unhappy, and fearful of our future. When we operate mostly from the spirit (from our soul), we are more likely to feel happier, more peaceful and powerful, with a greater trust in the process of life. Look at the list below and see if you can identify where you operate from the most—the ego or the soul.

Operating from the Ego or from the Soul
© Phoebe Hutchison 2012

When we operate from the soul, not ego, we feel united with humanity. All sense of competition, attempts to gain more power, to stand out, fade. Envy, revenge, and hatred become a thing of the past when we stop believing in a world of *us* versus *them*. When we love our neighbours, our fellow humans (without exception), life improves, for our neighbours are merely a mirror reflection of ourselves. As self-love is an integral part of success, when we indisputably love all our fellow humans, our self-love increases and we become a magnet for success!

Negative Thoughts (Ego)	Positive Thoughts (Soul)
Fake	Real self
Winner/loser	We are all kindred spirits
Nasty	Kind
Talk over someone	Listen to someone
Never satisfied	Constantly grateful
Hate/anger	Love
Selfish	Generous
Jealous	Admire
Blame	Forgive
Impatient	Patient
Enemies	Love for all humanity
Disgust	Empathy
Resentful	Let go and live in the present
Criticize	Praise
Pessimistic	Optimistic
Judge	Accept
Obsessed by success	Enjoy work, family and friends
Dishonest	Honest
Aggressive	Assertive
Self-doubt	Self-love and confidence
Fear	Faith in intuition and life!

Twelve-Circle Therapy—Understanding Your Issues
© Phoebe Hutchison 2013

We all experience difficult times, but we make it harder for ourselves when we suppress our feelings. If we push our issues aside without dealing with them, we may disown our associated emotions, and life could become more challenging. Our issues can often have many layers, many factors, and when we consider all of these we realize why we are so emotional about certain issues.

I have created Twelve-Circle Therapy, which is a great technique for ensuring we are considering all factors relating to each issue. This can be helpful for the following situations:

1. *Current Issues:* When you're contemplating current issues, such as trying to understand why you may be feeling stressed, overwhelmed, and over emotional on a particular day. Let's say you are having a bad day and are feeling irritated and

angry. The simple act of listing all the stressful, negative events may be enough to help you move forward and back to being positive again. Place a piece of paper on the desk, draw twelve circles, and then write a list of twelve issues (or as many as you can) that may be contributing to your negative emotions. Study the list. Acknowledge that these are stressful events, and then either visualize these events as balloons floating away in the sky, or simply rip up your list! Once you have released this negative energy, you can start again. Take a deep breath and begin your day again—with positive energy.

2. *Indecision:* Twelve-Circle Therapy is a great model for dealing with indecision. Firstly, being ready for change in our lives comes in stages. Are you contemplating change or happy with the way things are? Are you preparing for change and gathering the required information? Or are you ready for change now? Do you want change? Part of dealing with any decision is comprehending all the factors—physical, emotional, financial, and spiritual. Twelve-Circle Therapy works wonders for "drilling down" and understanding all the details. For example, you may wish to move. List all the reasons in your twelve circles (six circles *for* your decision and six circles *against*). Now review your list. What is your most important priority right now? By studying your list you should be closer to making a decision—and of course rely on your intuition as well when making a decision (see chapter 5).

3. *Past Issues:* When someone has suffered grief, loss, divorce, or separation, moved house, or been through a traumatic experience such as a car accident, house fire, violence, and more, Twelve-Circle Therapy can assist a person uncover all the contributing factors. Once all areas are considered, the person can gain greater understanding of the gravity,

complexity, and depth of his or her issues and can move forward toward healing. In many cases, professional assistance (with a counsellor or psychologist) is recommended for working with past issues as acknowledging past pain and loss can be complex, and you may become overwhelmed emotionally. A counsellor or psychologist can help a person with follow-up strategies, ensuring he or she is in a safe place to divulge, discuss, and list all areas affected by his or her traumatic situation.

Following is an example of how Janet was helped using this therapy.

Janet was not coping with life and said she had no idea why. She felt frozen, numb, and could not move forward or make big decisions. Janet appeared easy-going and smiled a lot, but I got the feeling that her happy-go-lucky attitude was a front for a deeper disappointment in life. I asked Janet to tell me what had been happening, to which she replied, "Nothing much." I then explained Twelve-Circle Therapy and asked her to simply tell me what was bothering her, in "machine-gun style," one after the other, as if her issues were just balloons she was holding in her hand.

What were her balloons?

1. She was lonely.
2. She had no friends.
3. She was angry toward her husband and felt like a prisoner.
4. She was not happy at her job.
5. She was stressed about her son.
6. She felt fat, as she had gained a lot of weight.
7. She felt useless, as her daughter was married now and she no longer felt needed.
8. She lacked confidence.

9. She had trouble standing up for herself at home and work.
10. She was suffering from depression and wanted to cut down on antidepressants as she felt lethargic and over-medicated.
11. She did nothing for herself and felt lost.
12. She could not find a twelfth issue (which is okay).

Used this way, Twelve-Circle Therapy has enabled Janet to move forward toward healing by increasing her understanding of all her issues. Once the issues were acknowledged, we put strategies in place so healing could begin and Janet could stop feeling stuck.

When we know an issue exists and *why* we feel the way we feel, when we understand our emotions and all the factors surrounding the issue, we are well on the way to solving that issue. Twelve-Circle Therapy can be used to identify all the factors related to a current issue including negativity on a day-to-day basis, indecision, a past traumatic event, grief, and more. Healing and acceptance often occur more rapidly after acknowledging our suffering.

Your Thoughts Run Deep—Unconscious Connection © Phoebe Hutchison 2013

Have you ever had an experience whereby something happened to you and suddenly you found yourself over-reacting? It's hard to understand, but something seemingly ordinary has set your heart pounding or drives you a little crazy. Well, it's time to stand back and ask yourself, "What is it about this situation? Why do I feel this way? Why is this experience making me feel so frustrated, anxious, fearful and angry (or any way that seems abnormal)?" Your emotions may be setting off alarm bells relating to a past event or set of events, something deeper in your unconscious mind.

Based on buried emotions of the past, I developed a technique I call The Unconscious Connection. Psychiatrist and psychotherapist Carl Jung, in *The Undiscovered Self,* indicates that our urges and behaviours are determined by what we have experienced in the past, among other things, and by our unconscious thoughts and emotions. These emotions drive us. Sometimes these experiences and emotions have been forgotten or suppressed, yet they are in our subconscious and control our current behaviour.

Sonya was having a shower, preparing for a night out with her girlfriends in the city when she suddenly felt terrified. Sonya felt surprised by her intense emotion. Surely she was safe. She went through the details in her mind. She would be with four friends, in a populated part of the city ... so why was she so scared? Confused by her worried state, she called one of her friends. Her friend asked if she had ever been through a traumatic experience when on a night out with girlfriends. It was then that Sonya recalled a horrifying night, more than twenty years before, when she was out with her girlfriends and a drunken fight ensued. It was a violent incident, involving the police, hospitalizations, counselling, and lasting trauma. Sonya now understood why she felt so scared. Her fear was an unconscious connection to similar past events. Her subconscious mind was trying to warn her because a previous trip to the city "with the girls" had ended very badly. Once Sonya realized the reason, she felt much calmer.

When you have an extreme reaction to something, someone, or an experience, attempt to really tap into this emotion. Is it an unconscious connection? What happened in the past that could be causing the current over emotional response? There may be a parallel situation causing you fear. Am I behaving irrationally? Am I over emotional? Unconscious connection is simply amazing self-therapy!

You See What You Think You See

A fascinating insight about the brain is that what we see is influenced by our thoughts. So what we think we see is different from person to person. Our interpretation of what we *see* is based on what we have seen and experienced in our life.

One example was when my son and I both witnessed the same car accident, yet we each saw it differently. We were standing in a parking lot when we heard a car speeding up. We turned and saw a car race around a nearby corner and then fly over a medium strip, onto the other side of the road, hitting a parked car and horse float and speeding off. We were absolutely shocked. My son and I discussed the accident on the way home and discovered we had two completely different opinions of what we had seen. I thought I had seen a car come around the corner, very fast, fishtailing in the wet. The driver seemed to be enjoying it but then lost control before flying over the medium strip, hitting the car and horse float before speeding off. My son's interpretation was a car came around the corner too fast, lost control, and slid to the left. The driver then tried to correct this by turning his steering wheel to the right before spinning out of control, crossing the medium strip in the centre of the road, hitting the parked car and horse float before driving off.

It was fascinating to discover that two people who had seen exactly the same thing had completely different interpretations. Our prejudices, opinions, and experiences, everything that goes into our brain—millions of impressions or thoughts influence what we see.

Daily Silence Will Transform Your World

Many years ago, I heard that one of the world's most famous female singers doesn't listen to music at home; instead, her home is silent. I found this hard to believe at the time, but nowadays I too am turning to daily silence. So many people wake up, prepare for work, rush off, put the radio on in the car, listen to the songs, the news, arrive at work, work all day (often through lunch), and arrive home. After preparing and eating dinner, they sit in front of the TV news, read the paper, watch the current-affairs program, watch the latest TV shows, talk to their family, prepare for bed, and try to go to sleep. It's no wonder so many people have trouble sleeping—they have not given themselves time to just sit, relax, analyze daily events, and think about the issues in their lives.

Give yourself the experience of daily silence and reap the many benefits of quiet time. When we introduce quiet time, we give our thoughts a chance to catch up. We are more able to step back, analyze our emotions, and interpret the events in our lives. When we are silent, we are more likely to have great inspirational thoughts; wonderful ideas flow through to us, such as ways in which we can improve our life at work and home. These benefits affect our performance during our daily tasks. Our stamina and productivity increase. Our stress levels reduce, improving our health, as we slow everything down. We become more grounded, and less distracted by the hectic pace of life, when we have daily silence, adding intensity to all of our relationships. Try driving the car without the radio on or taking a walk in the morning before work to give yourself time to think. Eat dinner without a TV blaring in the background.

If you are stressed, feeling frantic, confused, depressed, or angry often, pay attention to how much silence you have in your life. I'll bet you don't have a lot. Silence is our friend. There is a time for everything in life—a time for being busy and a time to reflect. Make silence part of your daily routine and notice the magical changes in every area of your life.

A friend recently visited for a short holiday. He thought we were strange, as we did not have the TV on during our meals or throughout the day. At his home, there is always a TV on in the background. So the following morning, he managed to find a news channel and we all sat staring at the TV over our breakfast. By the time the TV was switched off, I felt sad, frustrated, and a little angry. The news was all negative; a missing child, thousands of people in New Orleans had no power due to cyclones, and apparently young couples nowadays have to make a choice—baby or mortgage, due to increased costs of living. All this negativity first thing in the morning, seeping into my being, made me feel ill. Yet many people, from the time they wake until the time they go to sleep, let negative images and information constantly seep into their souls and brains.

Catch a Sleep Wave

Do you have trouble going to sleep? Here's a trick you can use. When you want to go to sleep, you need to catch a "sleep wave," a time when you feel sleepy. Sleep usually follows soon after. These sleep waves, as I call them, come periodically when we are tired and they last approximately ten minutes. In this period, we become drowsy, our muscles relax, our breathing slows, and our thoughts become vague. (Our brainwaves change from beta to alpha waves in preparation for sleep.) These sleep waves don't last long, so as soon as you feel a sleep wave come over you, quickly turn out the lights, and you should soon fall fast asleep.

While waiting for a sleep wave, read a book, chat quietly with your partner, or listen to soft music. Avoid asking yourself questions while trying to go to sleep, because the mind will respond by trying to find the answers. Your body will support your mind by keeping you awake in order to answer the questions. This works wonderfully well on long road trips when you want to stay awake but is terrible if you want to fall asleep. If you have things you need to think about, don't try to fall asleep. Get out of bed, grab your diary or a notepad, and do the mental work before going back to bed. Lying in bed with the lights out, thinking, will keep you awake longer and leave you feeling frustrated.

The Power of Meditation

Sometimes our minds can become overtired, like a toddler after a huge day. Our brain may be overstimulated by overthinking, or experiencing new things and challenges; we may meet new people, have long conversations or perform new roles at work. We can feel like a wound-up spring. When this happens, your mind is overworked. Enter the power of meditation.

Have you ever sat at a bus stop or train station watching the people walking by? Women and men in suits, couples and individuals all with their own style, all seemingly having a purpose, travelling from one place to another—some fast, others slow. Now, if we compare our minds to a busy train station, all these people are just like our different thoughts and impulses. Our mind is always being stimulated by what it is seeing, hearing, subconsciously thinking about, as well as what we are concentrating on. There are so many distractions. When we meditate, we give all those thoughts, rushing all over the brain, a chance to slow down. We give our brain a chance to focus on one thing and let all the constant activity in the mind slow down. Through the quiet mind, we are able to think more clearly and achieve greater peace.

Some people meditate by sitting in a chair, some lie on the floor and close their eyes for a few minutes, while others sit cross-legged and chant. We can quiet our minds in the car, on a train trip, a walk, a run, doing housework, Pilates, or yoga. Sometimes while working in my office, I achieve this state by simply mindlessly word processing and letting my busy mind relax. When you are in the present, and quieten everything down, you can find yourself in a very deep sense of relaxation. Sometimes just flipping open a magazine and having a read can be calming for the mind. All these things give the brain a chance to rest, and once rested, the brain can perform well, and the gut instinct, the spiritual side of us, can become more utilized.

Meditation can be done formally (or in the comfort of your home with a CD or DVD from a reputable practitioner), or by simply spending periods of time "zoning out."

Meditation has many advantages for our health and has been known to have the following benefits:

Health: Reduces blood pressure, improves stamina, reduces muscle tension, assists the immune system, helps the body heal, assists weight loss by keeping us grounded, reduces headaches, and improves general health.

Emotions: Reduces anxiety, promotes peace, improves self-confidence and autonomy, improves creativity, increases patience and self-control, and reduces aggressiveness.

Cognition: Improves memory, concentration, and problem-solving ability.

Spiritually: Assists in better mind/body connection, assists intuition, and increases sense of well-being, direction, and mindfulness.

A study at UCLA Laboratory of Neuro Imaging in California suggested that long-term meditation thickens grey matter, as well as increasing the number of folds in the cortex of the brain. As this area is believed to play a role in memory, thought, attention, and consciousness, one could conclude that long-term meditation improves brain functioning. By improving thought, we can improve our life, since much of our life is originated from our thoughts (http://newsroom.ucla.edu/portal/ucla/evidence-builds-that-meditation-230237.aspx, accessed 15/01/2014).

Homework—Are You Listening to Your Thoughts?

1. Regularly diarize your automatic thoughts. Understand and confront these internal messages.
2. When you have an upsetting experience, use the ABC model to reduce negative emotions.
3. Use Twelve-Circle Therapy to understand the many factors involved in stressful events, indecisions, or past traumatic experiences.
4. Create five positive affirmations for the most challenging areas in your life.
5. To be happy, aim for negative thoughts to be fleeting and positive thoughts to remain.
6. Irrational fears: When you are afraid, without reason, could this be an unconscious connection? Have you been through a similar experience in the past that is causing you to overreact now?

The physical organism, your body, has its own intelligence, as does the organism of every other life-form. And that intelligence reacts to what your mind is saying, reacts to your thoughts. So emotion is the body's reaction to your mind.—Eckhart Tolle

What you fear most is what will most plague you. Your fear will draw it to you like a magnet.—Neale Donald Walsch

CHAPTER 3

ARE YOU LISTENING TO YOUR EMOTIONS?

Why You Should Listen to Your Emotions

We all have trauma. We all go through painful times and live through moments of utter despair. Sometimes it feels like we are lost in the woods, darkness all around, with no way to escape our pain. Painful experiences usually lead to many negative thoughts, and from repeated negative thoughts we often become extremely emotional. This can make us unpredictable, irritable, sombre, difficult to live with, and usually challenging to work with. As part of unresolved negativity, we often omit a negative energy that can repel, irritate, or make others feel sorry for us.

We may also experience intense anger toward ourselves, others, and the world, further alienating us. We may have experienced a job loss, failed an exam, broken up with our partner, suffered a financial blow, or lost a loved one through death. We could feel as though our soul has taken a battering. We may feel ripped up inside or numb. Sometimes life is devastatingly cruel or unkind and we feel self-pity. These emotions serve to be a constant reminder, to warn us, so we can try to avoid repeating the painful experience. However, our emotions can become trapped, unresolved, taking years for us to heal, leaving us feeling unbalanced. Some people never heal and take this negativity to the grave. It absorbs them, destroys them, and as if by an unconscious wish, they become sick and eventually leave the world they experienced as cruel and cold.

The Power of Our Emotions

I like to think about emotions as a flow chart. It helps me, and it certainly helps my clients. Thoughts turn into emotions, which affect our bodies. Negative thoughts can lead to sickness and disease. Of course there are also positive results that can happen from positive emotions, but every thought we have registers in our body deeply, affects us, and becomes emotions. So it is a real chain of events, and accordingly it is important that we choose our thoughts carefully.

Dealing with Current Emotions

How can we decode, listen to our current negative emotions, and quickly move back to peace? Well, when working with clients, I recommend the Three Ws system to help my clients understand and work through their emotions. I use it for myself when I am feeling emotional and want to get through a difficult moment. If you are feeling emotional, flustered, angry, or out of control, ask yourself these three questions:

1. What am I feeling?
2. Why am I feeling this way?
3. What can I do about it right now that is positive and productive?

Now imagine you are single and it is Saturday night. You are home alone but would rather be out with company, and all of a sudden you feel very frustrated. If you ask yourself the above three questions, you will soon understand why you feel the way you do, which then allows you to make the necessary changes.

Your answers may be as follows:

1. I am feeling frustrated.
2. It's Saturday night and I am alone again. I am sick of being alone.
3. Call friends and see if anyone wants to go out. Go to the gym to improve confidence or body image. Join an Internet dating website. Make plans for next Saturday night as to not repeat this event. Go on Facebook and chat with a friend.

So often we feel emotional, but we do not know why. When we discover why and take action, we can quickly move through and out of these negative emotions.

Dealing with Unresolved Emotions

If we have deep, long-standing negative emotions, they can make us sick. How can we release them? While we should listen to our emotions, as they serve us as our own warning system, we benefit by becoming healed and whole again. How can we become healed? How can we deal, for example, with the lingering pain from divorce or anger at an ex-spouse, or how do we overcome guilt after an affair?

We need to:

1. Feel, face, and explore the pain.
2. Have increased awareness; process *all* the details around the surrounding events.
3. Release the negative emotions from within us.
4. Accept the events, forgive ourselves and others, and release all blame.

The residual emotion left will ensure we do not forget the lessons surrounding the trauma.

How Can We Help Ourselves?

We can all help ourselves by writing about our emotions in a diary, or by writing poems or songs. We can write letters and then burn them (not only to ensure they're never sent, but the act of burning can be cathartic). We can ensure that we fully understood the events, what we did, and what we failed to do. We can ask ourselves, "How can I learn from this experience?" We can talk to friends or family about our feelings. We can work through our thoughts and emotions with a counsellor or psychologist, or seek help from a natural-health practitioner or doctor. We can also explore natural remedies to assist the body becoming more in tune with the mind. Often it is the body that may be "out of balance," which can lead to us feeling over emotional and distressed.

How to Release Trapped Emotions

Professional counsellors use various techniques to help clients uncover and work with their thoughts and deep emotions. Gestalt therapy (developed by Fritz and Laura Perls and Paul Goodman in the 1940s and '50s) deals with deep emotions from past experiences that affect and impact our lives now. Various techniques are used to help the client move toward self-actualization by resolving past unresolved issues. In some cases, people may end up at impasse, unable to move forward or back and feeling completely stuck. By working with a therapist, they can be freed up and are able to "move" again. The therapist will encourage the clients to talk about feelings they are experiencing in the here and now.

The solution for a problem does not always have to be an answer. It can be helpful to simply have:

1. An increased awareness about how we feel and what the influencing factors are.
2. A different perception, so we can see how others involved may feel or have felt.
3. An emotional release so we can feel and release unexpressed pain and move forward to become much happier and feel lighter as we release negative emotions and heal.

If you feel like you have unfinished business that is negatively impacting your life, seek help from a psychologist or counsellor who ideally has Gestalt therapy training.

Change Channels

You take yourself wherever you go, so don't be cruel to yourself! Moving house, changing jobs, or getting divorced and/or remarried won't fix the issue or make you happy if *you* are the problem.

It is very easy to get into the habit of negative thinking. Thinking negative thoughts frequently will take you to the deeply saddened, and ultimately depressed zone, after a while. In these zones you use a lot of energy thinking about very dark subjects, which leaves you feeling disempowered. When I am with a client who is experiencing a lot of negative thinking, I often use CBT (cognitive behaviour therapy, as discussed earlier) to help adjust his or her thoughts. However, another technique is to visualize the waves of thoughts that go through our brains as similar to a television channel. When we are fed up with our negative self-talk, we can simply visualize changing from the negative-thoughts channel to the positive-thoughts channel.

I first began using this concept many years ago. I would wake up, look in the mirror, and the "self-attacks" would begin. I would be negative about my weight, hair, skin, teeth, and myself in general. This time was all about being nasty to myself. I decided to change channels and made a decision to think only positive and kind thoughts while preparing for the day. It took a few weeks, but I managed to change channels, and my mornings became beautiful again, instead of a bitch session against myself (a terrible way to start any day!).

Mornings are so sacred. Do you start the day off being kind to yourself, or nasty? It takes twenty-one days to change a habit, so go ahead and change channels today!

How to Deal with Angry Energy

I was watching a reality TV show recently, where a fashion model was getting teased by a group of other models. And the model who was getting harassed *just took it.* She didn't speak back or stand up for herself. She just became silent but looked more and more upset, sorry for herself, and flustered. This abuse and provocation from the models continued as they were getting their makeup done and getting dressed. Finally, as they were about to start a photo-shoot, the model who was continually being harassed exploded. She was holding a tray of drinks, and she threw them to the side and ran straight toward the main girl who had been teasing her and attempted to strangle her. She had a meltdown and flew into an angry, out-of-control rage, and this to me summarized anger and violence. If we do not take steps to ensure our continued peace, we are all capable of losing control. This model could have ignored the comments and used positive self-talk, or assertively stood up for herself and told the main antagonist to back off in a controlled yet assertive way. Instead, she bottled up her anger and then lost control. Anger, like many emotions, wants to be free. It is better for us to be assertive and use positive self-talk and remain calm than to become filled with rage and spiral out of control.

The following is a great exercise that highlights causes of stress and your reactions to it. First, draw a volcano on a piece of paper, taking up the bottom half the page. Next, write on the sides of the volcano, moving up the page toward the top, everything that stresses you, the triggers—all the things that make you feel angry or stressed. Put the least stressful things at the bottom and the most stressful things at the top. My list would include too much happening at once, my child nagging me in a shop, running late, being lost while driving, or not being able to find my mobile phone.

Now use the top part of the page to draw the volcano erupting. Next to the lava spewing out the top, write a list of your reactions to these stresses, making the higher ones your most intense reactions and the lower ones your smaller reactions. My reactions may be feeling flustered, not being able to concentrate, and being short-tempered.

Part of anger management is recognizing the external signs and events that contribute to the anger. Another part of anger management is to recognize the signs in our bodies; signs like sweaty palms, our heart beating faster, our mind feeling racy, our breathing changing, or feeling a burst of energy as the adrenalin kicks in. Our body is preparing us for fight or flight. *Our body is preparing us for conflict or to run away.*

Let anger be the fleeting emotion in you, not the one that stays. Happiness is being free of constant anger.

Are You Addicted to Anger?

We can become accustomed to the same emotional responses, and our brains can become "addicted" to certain chemical changes and responses in our bodies. Different emotions elicit different chemical reactions. If you are in love, your body produces endorphins that give you the "lovers high." Similarly, our emotions convert into chemical reactions, which make emotional states habitual, the same way drinking a high-energy drink or having a cappuccino can become a habit, and gives you a surge of energy as a reaction to the caffeine. In much the same way, some people develop the habit of becoming angry; you could almost say they are addicted to anger. They may continually use the adrenalin from being angry to "get things done."

When people are addicted to anger, they seem to constantly find things that make them angry. They get into the habit of being irritated by their surroundings, which causes an increase of energy as their bodies prepare them for fight or flight with adrenalin, increased blood rushing through the body, and a faster heart rate. Of course these people would be hard to work with and certainly hard to live with. It is also damaging for a person's health to be constantly angry. The adrenal glands become overworked, the body can become fatigued, and sickness can result. Adrenalin is only meant to be a short-term solution, not a lifestyle. So how do we get out of the anger habit?

Changing the Anger Habit

In order for us to stop the anger cycle, we need to *stop* everything we are doing and change what's happening. Can we change the environment? If we can't—we can *walk away!* We can delay! (Make a time to discuss later.) Can we be assertive without being aggressive? Can we say something to end the conversation assertively without aggression? Can we agree to disagree? What can we do to make a difference *now*, so we do not lose control? We can visualize calming down, walking away, taking deep breaths, and counting to ten. We can use self-talk to minimize our reaction. Visualizing a calm reaction to stressful situations will help, and removing ourselves from the situation gives us time to calm our body down.

Anger not dealt with can easily become resentment, which destroys relationships and inner peace. Anger turned inward can lead to, or contribute towards, depression. Anger that is out of control is called rage. When we are angry, it motivates us to act. So we can calm down and then be assertive by discussing our needs, feelings, and thoughts. If we attempt to discuss our thoughts while angry, we risk saying things we may regret, or even worse, becoming violent.

Anger is a normal response, but frequent anger is not good for our health. We all feel anger. It is important how we react to this emotion. Often this emotion is an indicator that a need is not being met, that we are exhausted, working too hard, feeling violated, ignored, or disrespected, just to name a few. When we have calmed down, we need to understand what triggered the anger so we can make changes to try to avoid a repeat episode. We can use anger as an indicator rather than a motivator. We can listen to anger and make the changes in our life to reduce it. *Anger talks to us.*

We can also take steps to ensure we are less likely to react in anger. Steps such as meditation, relaxation therapy, and exercising—anything we can do to reduce our knee-jerk reactions to stressful events. There will always be stressful events; we just need to be ready for them and learn how to handle them better. When we understand more about the triggers that make us angry and how we react, we can then spend time thinking of more appropriate reactions to stressful situations. By doing so, we reduce stress in our lives. Instead of feeling as though anger is controlling us, we can simply use anger as guidance, a tool.

What is your anger really telling you about your life?

Remove Yourself and Remain Calm

Sandra was enjoying another beautiful, family Christmas gathering at her house. All her family were relaxing with full bellies after the delicious feast. Her relatives sat in a circle, talking about "the good old days." Sandra made a comment about her father and her childhood, and suddenly, Sandra's aunty Joanne began yelling at her. "How dare you! Do you have any idea what your father went through when you were growing up?" Sandra felt attacked by this outburst. She felt as though her aunty Joanne had just punched her in the stomach. Sandra was shaking and felt ready to verbally retaliate as her body filled with adrenalin. But it was Christmas!

Even though Sandra felt wronged, she stood up calmly and assertively said, "Excuse me, Aunty Joanne, I need to remove myself from your aura." Sandra moved and sat a few seats away from her aunty. Sandra took a couple of deep breaths and was able to regain control both physically and emotionally and gain some distance in perspective. In this position, she was able to decide that an argument was pointless and would spoil such a lovely day. Sandra calmed her body and mind down. She reflected on the situation and made a decision to avoid unnecessary conflict at this time.

Don't Be Connected by Angry Energy

Have you ever been really angry with someone and fumed and stewed about their words, thought about what you'd like to say to that person but haven't said it? When you see this person there is negative energy, but still nothing is said to clear the air.

I once had this experience with a workmate. I can't even remember what started it, but I was angry with her and was pretty sure she was angry with me. We'd be at work and I'd say something and just the way she'd reply would let me know she was not happy. Then when I'd leave work I'd think about it for hours and become upset and angry. This went on for a few days until I bumped into her outside of work and confronted her about the tension. I told her how I felt. She started crying and then I felt like crying, but we talked it through and moved on. It was a miscommunication and we were friends again. The "psychic tennis match" was over. Yet it had been so powerful and so destructive for a few days.

It is so easy to play but so incredibly destructive. This anger, from both sides, connects us. While this angry link is unhealthy and maladjusted, it is very real. In spiritual warfare we are linked to the people we are angry with. So many people in this world are divorced and are linked in anger. Do you want to be spiritually connected with an ex-partner or a person you cannot stand? We need to cut those invisible ties by changing the emotion. When the emotion moves from a dark cloud of negativity to an acceptance of the situation, the invisible bond will weaken. Ultimately, we can move on to letting the person go with love, and part of this process is forgiveness and part may be releasing unspoken words. You may need to visualize a giant pair of scissors cutting the link, and then release the person with love.

If we are angry with just one person, it affects our whole life. That negative energy affects every part of our being. It is not possible for us to be a ball of pure love, and to love our life and everyone in it, if we are angry at even one person. It ripples through our being. If you find yourself angry with anyone at all, be aware that this can make you sick, and it will rob you of your potential. Forgiveness and letting the emotions out, in a healthy way, is the key. Work with a therapist (a counsellor or psychologist) if you wish, diarize your feelings, or write poems. Do whatever you can to release that energy. You may need to scream into a cushion, hit your mattress using a pillow, buy a punching bag, or start an exercise routine, such as brisk walking, to release angry energy. Maybe you need to say something to the person you are angry with; tell him or her how much he or she has hurt you—and then let the anger go. Do whatever it takes to make sure that inside you, there is no connection to another in anger. Connecting in anger will affect your life detrimentally. Connecting in love is what we want.

Depression—Take Back Your Power!

Depression is epidemic in society. According to the World Health Organization, more than 350 million people of all ages suffer from depression, globally. Depression is the leading cause of disability worldwide, and is a major contributor to the global burden of disease. (http://www.who.int/mediacentre/factsheets/fs369/en/, accessed 10/01/2014).

Of the seventy thousand thoughts we have per day, how would we feel if the majority of these were negative? According to American psychiatrist Aaron Beck, a depressed person views himself or herself as deficient/inadequate/deserted. Depression is a state where you have high self-blame and low self-concept and you compare yourself unfavourably to others. This leads to self-rejection, of negative views of yourself and your future. You feel helpless, lack motivation, may have suicidal thoughts, or begin to think others would be better off without you. The physical signs of depression include fatigue, agitation, loss of libido, sleep disturbances, crying spells, escaping life, and avoiding work and friends. You feel life is futile and are highly self-critical. Everything is difficult, life is too hard, and pleasure and satisfaction are rare.

If you have depression, you will benefit by having a purpose, doing positive activities, seeing a therapist, working with affirmations, using a diary, and understanding your emotions and thoughts. You will benefit by visiting a doctor to see if he or she recommends medication (to use in conjunction with strategies and therapy). There are new medications constantly being developed to help with depression. Science explains that antidepressants create changes in the brain by addressing chemical imbalances.

How Do I See Myself and My Life?

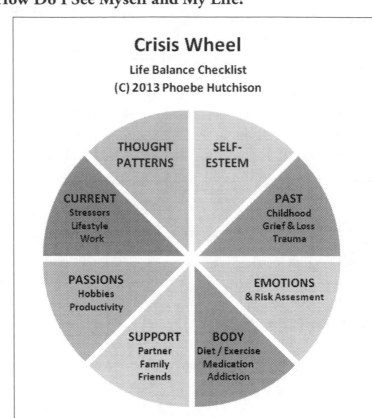

Crisis Wheel

Life Balance Checklist
(C) 2013 Phoebe Hutchison

THOUGHT PATTERNS

SELF-ESTEEM

CURRENT
Stressors
Lifestyle
Work

PAST
Childhood
Grief & Loss
Trauma

PASSIONS
Hobbies
Productivity

EMOTIONS
& Risk Assesment

SUPPORT
Partner
Family
Friends

BODY
Diet / Exercise
Medication
Addiction

The Crisis Wheel © Phoebe Hutchison 2013

I developed the crisis wheel as a therapeutic tool to quickly identify the extent of a client's issues at initial assessment, and then later to evaluate progress. The crisis wheel is helpful when working with anyone who has been diagnosed with depression or having issues such as separation distress, chronic indecision, self-harm, anxiety, addiction, grief and loss, and more. It is holistic in approach, and therefore all areas of a person's life are considered, such as self-esteem, past trauma, grief and loss, emotional imbalance and risk assessment, diet, exercise, medications, addiction, support available to client, client passion and productivity, stressors in lifestyle (including work), and thought patterns. After using the crisis wheel, strategies can be given to enable healing and personal growth in the specific areas. This ensures therapy can be most effective as it is delivered in the shortest amount of time for the fastest recovery and personal growth.

Some clients may be experiencing issues in only a few areas, while others are struggling with many (or all) areas. A client may present in my counselling rooms as deeply saddened and not coping, yet assessment indicates he or she is satisfied at work, the person exercises, has great friendships, and is a conscientious parent … the client is missing one thing: an emotional connection to his or her spouse, resulting in feelings of rejection, loneliness, and desperation. Once the client learns assertiveness and relationship-strengthening strategies, his or her life quickly becomes balanced again. This therapy is fast because strategies are applied directly where they are needed.

In contrast, if clients present in my counselling rooms with low motivation and high self-criticism (low self-esteem), no friends, no intimate relationships (no social supports), they feel like the world is against them (negative thought patterns), they don't like their boss, are unhappy at work (lifestyle/work unhappiness), do not exercise (body: not enough endorphins—"feel-good chemicals" in the brain), are still furious over their divorce (past trauma and unresolved grief and loss), and feel constantly angry at an ex-partner (emotions out of balance), I consider these clients to be in extreme crisis. Their issues are deep and cover all areas. These clients may be at risk of suicide, and I would encourage frequent counselling sessions in the beginning weeks, along with a plethora of helpful strategies. I also ensure the clients are equipped with phone numbers and supports to keep them safe and to encourage healing and self-growth as fast as possible.

Feel free to use this crisis wheel to gain greater clarity and another perspective on your issues and your life. This crisis wheel will enable you to see the areas in which you may be stuck or need some help, and the areas in your life that are going well. If you need help in many areas, please seek help from a doctor, psychologist, or counsellor.

Self-Esteem

Do you no longer like or respect yourself? Are you often self-critical, filled with self-doubt? Do you have low confidence and poor motivation? Make a list of your strengths and achievements in life—everything you like about yourself. (If this was difficult, you may have low self-esteem.) Low self-esteem can be the result of childhood abuse, neglect, being in a dysfunctional family or relationship, allowing others to treat you poorly, and/or having a lot of negative thoughts about yourself. Your self-esteem is vital for you to have self-confidence, high motivation, and independence, which creates a solid foundation for success in life personally and professionally. Low self-esteem has been linked to feelings of inadequacy, guilt, insecurity, high self-blame (and blaming others), and frequently feeling like a failure. Using the strategies in this book, you can change your subconscious (underlying thoughts about yourself) and improve your self-esteem.

The Past

Do you feel like you are "stuck in the past"? Do you seem to be constantly going over past events in your mind? Do you feel like a victim, like life has given you a "bad deal"? Do you have trouble letting go and forgiving others? Do your unhappy experiences, such as arguments, traumas, or losses feel like they are clouding your thoughts every day?

Make a list of any trauma, abuse, or losses you have experienced in your childhood or adult life that you feel you have not dealt with or resolved, issues that are still very much in your thoughts. This list may include, for example, childhood abuse, neglect, fears, a divorce, separation, the loss of a job, financial status, or death of a loved one.

We all suffer hardship and trauma. Sometimes we need a little help to let go, heal, and then move forward. With grief and loss, for instance, we are able to move forward in healing to eventual acceptance only after we have fully felt our feelings, our emotions, during the grief process, which takes time. If we look away, if we try to run from the grief process and deny what we have lost, we cannot fully incorporate the loss into our souls, and this keeps us looking back and not looking forward. Our mind will want us to think about our loss, as the mind needs to work toward resolution. While it is painful, a large part of grief and loss is focused remembering, paying attention to our pain, and experiencing the emotions that accompany profound loss. Healing happens after the hurt has been fully felt.

Emotions and Risk Assessment

Do you keep your feelings to yourself? Do you have conversations over and over in your mind but do not stand up for yourself? Do you often feel jealous, insecure, or frustrated? Does every day feel the same, like life is not exciting anymore and has lost its fun? Have you lost touch with your feelings, wants, and needs, and feel numb? Do you often say, "I couldn't be bothered ..."? Do you find that you are frequently feeling over emotional, angry, or some other negative emotion, which may include self-loathing? *Do you entertain thoughts of suicide? If you do, please seek help today.*

Call Lifeline, consult a doctor, see a therapist as soon as possible. Suicidal thinking is a sign you are in a serious emotional crisis, often impacting many areas in your life. Help is available, so please seek professional help and get supported immediately, so life can become enjoyable again.

The Body

Have you put on weight, and do you rarely exercise? Do you have trouble getting out of bed in the morning? Has your sex drive decreased? Do you take medications that may affect brain function? Do you drink alcohol frequently or binge drink? Do you take recreational drugs? Do you have low motivation and constantly feel lethargic?

A healthy diet and exercise routine play an important role in the health of the brain function, which impacts our moods and attitudes. Science supports the fact that depression is related to a chemical imbalance in the brain. We now know that recreational drugs change chemicals in the brain, and therefore many have been linked with depression.

So how can we improve the "cocktail" of chemicals in our brain? Exercise decreases cortisol, the "stress hormone" and increases serotonin, the "happy hormone," while releasing endorphins, nature's "feel–good" chemicals, which can give us a feeling of euphoria, reduce the sensation of pain, and increase our sense of calm and well-being. Exercise also releases adrenalin and dopamine, the "reward hormone" (which, if in short supply, can create low libido, low desire, aggression, weight gain, depression, poor attention, and ADHD).

A healthy diet can also improve the balance of these brain chemicals, improving our mood, memory, motivation, sex drive, feelings of well-being, sensitivity to pain, reduction in aggression, and more. While a "cure" for depression is still not here, science says serotonin and dopamine levels play a significant role, as they relate to reward, reinforcement, and motivation. Chemicals in the brain, the neurotransmitters, play a vital role in our mental health, and we influence these chemicals daily with our eating, exercise, and habits.

Support Networks

Do you feel socially unsupported, isolated, with few (or no) close friends? Are your relationships strong, or do you allow others to manipulate you, belittle you, or make decisions for you? Do you feel suffocated and controlled by someone? Are you in the habit of only caring for others, ignoring your own needs? Have you stopped standing up for your rights?

To feel strong in life, we need to have strong and healthy relationships. These relationships are ideally our shelter during life's storms. Research shows that being happily involved in a loving relationship increases our levels of oxytocin, the "love hormone," which makes us feel more relaxed and more attached to our loved ones. However, having poor relationships can be harmful to our self-esteem and our happiness and can throw our lives into turmoil. Sometimes life may seem challenging when all we really need is the strengthening of our relationships, with new strategies, including assertiveness. If your relationships are doing you more harm than good, seek new strategies and professional help.

Your Passions

Do you spend time on your goals, hobbies, or passions? Do you spend time thinking about what you want out of life, or do you feel like there is no time for you? Do you feel as if life is just work, work, work, with no time to relax? Do you sometimes have inspiration, but negativity stops you from following your passions? When do you feel powerful in your life?

For us to be truly happy, we need to feel empowered and inspired. We need to have hobbies and passions. For some people, work is their passion and they feel great power, satisfaction, and productivity. For other people life is simply work, pay the bills, and "plug into" the television at night. They do not feel a sense of satisfaction, power, or thrill over anything they do. Therefore, they do not have passion in their life, which creates an imbalance. Without having our own internal drive to achieve, life can seem to have little meaning. If you are not actively pursuing your passions, make changes today. Passion in our life is the fire in our soul that inspires us, motivates us to change, and keeps us strong through the storms of life.

Current Stressors

Are you unemployed, or do you find your work unsatisfying? Do you work at a job where you give everything and then neglect yourself? Does your job make you unhappy? Do you have a lot of stressors, such as financial pressure, sickness, children with disabilities, or anything that is taking your attention away from enjoying life? Is your life unbalanced? If you are unhappy at work, if your life has become unbalanced, or if you have a lot of pressures in your current life, it makes it difficult to focus on creating a wonderful life. What is not working in your life? What could be improved? Do you need better strategies to enable you to deal with your current stressors? Examine your life to determine which stressors can be reduced or eliminated and then make the required changes.

Thought Patterns

Do you worry a lot about the future? Do you feel helpless, like life has no point? Do you constantly criticize yourself and your efforts? Do you often find yourself thinking angry or negative thoughts? Are many of your thoughts focused on negative past events or worrying about upcoming events? Do you find that you don't often "live in the moment"?

Negative thinking is a habit that can begin in childhood. Our thinking patterns are also influenced by our friends, family, workmates, our self-esteem, and the shows and books we watch and read. Negative thinking can be changed, but it may take weeks of effort. Use the tools in this book, and perhaps work with a counsellor or psychologist, if negative thinking is having a detrimental impact on your daily life.

Help is available. You do not need to suffer alone. Seek help, get some strategies from a counsellor, psychologist, or doctor. In a crisis, call Lifeline (Australia) anytime: www.lifeline.org.au. Phone: 13 11 14. Everyone does care. You are worth it. There is help, so call out.

Depression—Watch For the "Warning Signs"

If you know someone who is depressed, it is important to keep listening in case he or she discusses thoughts around self-harm or suicide. When a person feels he or she has lost control or feels profound and long-standing negative emotions, the person may feel socially isolated or may show the warning signs of potential suicide (such as making a will, planning a funeral, saying good-bye, writing letters, giving possessions away, not talking, showing low enthusiasm for life, feeling negative about everything, etc.). *Seek professional help from a doctor, psychologist, or counsellor, or call Lifeline, if you notice these signs.* Professionals will assist your loved ones to focus on their strengths, normalize their anger, and help them make plans for the future that inspire them, plans designed to make them "linked to life" again, based on their interests. Medication may be required to help them feel happy again.

Don't Be Destroyed by Guilt

We are not meant to walk this earth with daily guilt. I feel incredibly emotional when I think about how life-destroying guilt can be. We all feel negative emotions. We all experience moments of anger, guilt, frustration, self-pity, and bitterness. These emotions teach us about our lives and our choices. They are a result of our thoughts and experiences. While we cannot stop negative emotions, we want them to be fleeting and our positive emotions to be constant. Guilt is a strong negative emotion, and it often makes a person suffer and feel persecuted. Guilt is a common part of the grief and loss process. It is hard enough to lose someone, or something important and valued in our life, but to then be consumed by guilt is an added burden. Guilt contributes to low self-esteem, helplessness, dissatisfaction with self, and unhappiness. Like any negative emotion, guilt can make people feel emotionally unbalanced, which usually negatively impacts their lives and relationships.

So why do you persecute yourself? Let it go. *You* need to forgive yourself, and you need to feel forgiven. If you believe in living mindfully, moment by moment, release this guilt now—as now does not need to be clouded with negative emotions from the past. In this moment, are you doing anything that could cause you to feel guilt? Guilt is an attack on your self-esteem. Guilt is the flag post—a simple warning—maybe you did something "wrong": you may have messed up, hurt someone, broke something, caused an unpleasant event, forgot to say something, or forgot to do something. Are you really to blame? If you knew then what you know now, would you have done what you did? No! Learn from the mistakes, and leave them in the past. Leave guilt in the past. Forgive yourself and forgive others. Do not let guilt destroy you.

Guilt left unchecked will fester in your soul and could contribute to depression and unhappiness. Guilt is like a red light, alerting us, telling us to stop and think ... and then we need to move forward again. It is not meant to be a life sentence. We cannot live a harmonious, joy-filled peaceful existence if we live with daily guilt. If you feel guilty about anything, *let it go.* Imagine it is in a balloon flying up into the sky and then bursting. Let these negative feelings be released from your soul. If you cannot let go of your guilt, please seek help from a psychologist or counsellor.

The Fear Trap

Fear keeps us living a responsible life, and fear keeps us alive, as it can stop us from doing dangerous things. However, fear can be devastating to our peace. Fear is like salt. A little bit of salt is good for you, but too much can be harmful and destroy your health. We can experience fear over so many things. We can have fear of the future, the unknown, a relationship breaking down, our loved ones dying, our success ending, natural catastrophes, being alone, failure, and poverty and illness, just to name a few.

Fear is a powerful emotion, and just as like attracts like, fear can attract a focus on fear! Just like any powerful emotion, fear can cause you to become sick. Fear can also cause what you fear to come true. Consider this universal law: "What you focus on expands." If you focus on your fears, these fears are more likely to happen. If you are stressed or worried that your business may fail, your energy and your head space is all focused on a negative "goal," so to speak. This could result in the fear being realized, as all your energy and attention is going toward that negative outcome. However, a little fear is healthy. If you are fearful of being poor, you could invest, save, and have financial strategies in place. It is always better for your energy, attention, and emotions to go into ways to improve your life and create more success!

Fear can be like a little person sitting on your shoulder, always ensuring you don't have any peace. This is not healthy. We can only do our best, and then we need to let go. We benefit by doing the following with fear:

1. Listen to the fear (e.g., I am fearful my son may take drugs),
2. Take action (e.g., educate him on the dangers of taking drugs, support him, love him, let him know he can talk to you),
3. Let go of the fear (e.g., it is your son's life and you have advised and educated him. He has common sense and intuition. Keep communication lines open).

Do You Blame Others for Your Life?

Having a good sense of personal power can make you feel in control and in charge. Yet many people give their power away to bosses, children, spouses, and negative thinking. Millions of people feel they are not in charge of their own lives; they feel powerless. This feeling of powerlessness can lead to low self-esteem and addictions to drugs, alcohol, or gambling. People may become self-abusive or violent or may overspend. People who feel they have no power may become angry, resentful, and develop disease. We humans are meant to feel powerful in our worlds. Having a perceived lack of power in our lives can lead to stress, maladjustment, deep sadness, depression, and mental illness. Take *your* power back!

Self-Loathing—Stop the Vicious Cycle

If everything amazing in life stems from healthy self-love, what stems from self-loathing? How does this even happen? Why do some people despise themselves? What happens to their world when they do?

We all get angry, disappointed, and frustrated with ourselves from time to time. We often have high expectations, and when we let ourselves down, we can have harsh internal dialogues. Yet self-loathing is more than this. It happens when people get into the negative habit of constantly putting themselves down, letting others put them down, spending time with people who make them feel terrible, allowing themselves to be abused, or eating or drinking in excess and then criticizing themselves for their appearance. They begin to look in the mirror and not like what they see, so they stop caring. They criticize themselves so much in their own mind that they believe everyone else dislikes them. As they have little or no confidence due to the constant mind criticisms, they do not speak up for themselves and instead may become violent as frustration builds, or they may drink excessively or take drugs to escape this self-hatred, and then they get angry at themselves.

These people put up with negative people, relationships, situations, accommodations, workplaces, and more, as they feel they deserve the worst life has to give, and even if this belief is subconscious, it will still show in their life. They often feel guilt for not meeting their parents', partner's, or their own expectations, or for their negative habits. They may feel guilt over a past event and not be able to forgive themselves. Often this negative cycle begins with low self-esteem or from poor parenting during childhood. And sadly, many self-loathers end up with depression. This may be partly caused through negative thoughts and circumstances, and/or a perceived lack of control.

Depression may also be caused by social drug use and the negative impact on the brain. The self-loather can change, but they need to plant flowers (affirmations) in their brain to compete against the weeds (negative thoughts). Little by little these people need to praise themselves, accept themselves, love themselves, accept their past actions, and forgive themselves. They need to work at changing their relationships and their situations to match this new level of self-love and respect, so that the new and loving inner world is reflected in their outer world.

Self-love is so much better. Self-love starts with self-talk— *every* word must be kind. No more of the following self-talk: "You idiot! What is wrong with you? You are useless. Everyone would be better off without you. You will never be a success. You are different from everyone else. No one could love you. You will be alone all your life. You are ugly. You are fat. You are stupid." *Stop it!* Say only kind things to and about yourself—and watch your life transform. *Everything* amazing in life starts with great self-esteem (self-love). If you need some help changing your mindset, consult a therapist, such as a counsellor, psychologist, or doctor. Life is so much better when we love ourselves.

How to Cope with Grief and Loss

We can experience grief as a result of a number of things. Grief could be a reaction to the death of a friend, family member, or spouse, or the loss of a relationship, job, financial status, or house. Grief can also be related to a perceived loss, such as loss of youth, beauty, strength, or independence. Grief can prove to be more difficult if we have previously experienced unresolved grief in our lives, as this further compounds our losses. Grief affects us all differently. Grief takes a very serious toll on our bodies and can even make us sick. During grief we may experience loss of appetite, fatigue, emotional numbness, have trouble sleeping, have trouble concentrating, and our mind may often be in "question mode," trying hard to find the answers— endlessly asking questions. "Why did this happen? What am I supposed to do now?"

There are different types of grief, some healthy and some unhelpful. There is standard grief, unresolved or anticipatory grief, and complicated grief (absent, inhibited, delayed, conflicted, chronic, unanticipated, and abbreviated). Loss has two parts; first you experience the loss, and then you have to do "the grief work" to ensure you are moving toward eventual acceptance.

According to Elisabeth Kübler-Ross and David Kessler, as outlined in their book, *On Grief and Grieving: Finding the Meaning of Grief Through the Five Stages of Loss,* most people who grieve pass through these five stages in no particular order: denial, anger, bargaining, depression, and acceptance. This book has proven to be very helpful for those experiencing grief, as it sheds light on the process.

Losing a loved one or suffering a loss is so incredibly painful, and the natural reaction we humans want is to escape pain. Yet in grief we need to face the pain. It helps to talk about the loss and incorporate it into our lives. When we try and shut out the loss, when we try to move on with life as if nothing has happened, our grief becomes more complicated and can take longer to work through. The ideal "healer" when dealing with grief and loss is *time* (as time does heal so much); nonetheless, we also need to work through the pain, with the eventual goal being acceptance.

Grief Work

To help us work through grief, we can use many of the following techniques:

Use of symbols: Use photographs or video to share thoughts about our loved one.

Writing: We can write to the lost loved one. We can write unspoken words, feelings, and thoughts in a diary.

Drawing: We can draw pictures of how we are feeling. (This is particularly good for children.)

Cognitive restructuring: With the help of a counsellor, we can test any unhelpful thoughts for accuracy.

Memory book: We can help integrate the loss by creating a book of stories, events, and memorabilia.

Directed imagery: Talk to the loved one. Sit opposite an empty chair and with eyes closed, visualize the loved one and talk to him or her. This is a very powerful technique and can be done with or without a counsellor.

Do Not Suffer in Silence—Help Is Available

Self-help books are fabulous. I have been reading them for more than twenty years. Nonetheless, sometimes you simply need to consult a psychologist or a counsellor, to dig deeper and experience more healing at a faster rate. Make sure your counsellor or psychologist is part of an ethical organization and is fully trained. Your counsellor or psychologist will most likely do the following:

- help you view your life and interactions realistically;
- assist in your growth, help you achieve your goals, give you strategies and homework;
- increase your awareness of your emotions and situations;
- help you think more positively;
- identify your strengths so you can work toward autonomy (working independently);
- encourage you to be congruent by confronting discrepancies in your actions, thoughts, and goals;
- help reframe your experiences in a more objective and positive way;

- normalize your emotions;
- help you to understand your subconscious, motivations and thoughts a little more; and
- show you how to identify irrational thoughts, change them, and reduce their frequency.

And lots more …

From the depths of your despair, from your lowest point, feel comfort in knowing that the only way is up. Take action and allow the healing to begin. We all have dark days, dark times … you are not alone in your sorrow. Miraculous transformations often occur to those in their darkest hour.

Homework—Are You Listening to Your Emotions?

1. Are you listening to anger?
   a. Do the volcano exercise (See paragraph How to Deal with Angry Energy) to learn more about your triggers and responses to stress and anger.
   b. Notice the way your body changes when you are angry. These messages should alert you to your emotional intensity, so you can respond calmly and assertively while remaining in control.
   c. What new strategies have you learned for keeping calm in potentially stressful situations?
   d. Are you connected by anger with anyone? Release blame, forgive, and enjoy more peace and happiness.
2. Depression: What are the symptoms of depression? What thoughts, life situations, and chemical changes have been discussed as possible factors in depression?
3. Crisis wheel: Do the self-evaluation exercise and learn more about yourself and your life. Discover which areas in your life need improvement and which areas are going well.

4. Practice "changing channels" from negative to positive, and watch as your life improves.
5. What are you *still* feeling guilty about? Make a list. Acknowledge, forgive, and then let go of guilt.
6. List all your fears. Use the exercise in this chapter to reflect on your fears. How likely are these fears to eventuate? What steps can you make, right now, that will make you feel safe? We need to listen to our fear, take action, and then *let go*.

*Medical researchers at such institutions as John Hopkins
University School of Medicine, the University of Southern
California, and Yale University are agreeing that emotions are
the primary factor in illness. And in tracking a disease from
its manifest state back through the body to the mental distress
that set off the physical imbalance, they are finding deep-seated
patterns of anxiety, grief, anger, depression, and fear. In thousands
of case histories the evidence is clear: the body does reflect the
state of an individual's emotions.*—John Randolph Price

*No group is at higher risk for depression, disease, and
early death than people who are completely sedentary,
and by now the value of regular exercise for all age groups
has been well documented.*—Deepak Chopra

CHAPTER 4

ARE YOU LISTENING TO YOUR BODY?

Be Grateful to Your Body

Your body is made up of billions and billions of atoms, each having its own nucleus, constantly in a state of motion, and interacting like billions and billions of little brains. Be astounded by the miracle that is your body; say kind things about your body. Your body, your vessel, is always listening and constantly being changed by your thoughts.

I am sure that most people have stood in front of the mirror, at some time or another, and been critical—I know I have. Have you ever noticed that people who seem to hate their bodies (people who abuse the mirror about their appearance and do not honour their bodies) seem to be at war with their bodies? They are the ones angrily looking down at the extra flab on their stomach and talk about this extra padding as though someone came and made them bigger. If we overeat, eat high-calorie foods, or drink too many high-calorie, sugary drinks, the body stores the extra energy (in our thighs or waist, etc.). Yet some people are disappointed with their bodies, but our bodies simply store this potential energy for us.

The biggest lesson I learned about body image came when I heard about a girl who had lost both her legs in an accident. She said she wished she had appreciated her legs more. She felt sad because she would previously say unkind words about her legs and her body, and now that she was left without legs, she truly wished she had been grateful for these wonderful limbs. So we should thank our skin, our bones, our organs, our eyes, our limbs, our hair ... they all work together to provide the framework that is our vehicle through life.

Help Your Body Serve You

A body is like a car. Going to the gym (or working out at home) is like having your car serviced. We need to look after it so it can serve us well. Exercise is not just about being fit and/or losing weight; exercise is about helping the lungs and heart strengthen. Exercise helps the body move lymphatic fluid around, heal the body, and move fresh, oxygenated blood where it is needed. Exercise increases the feel good chemicals (neurotransmitters) in the brain, such as serotonin, dopamine, and endorphins. Increasing these chemicals has been shown to help improve sleep, the thought process, regulate emotions, and increase our pain threshold (physically and emotionally). It is no wonder that exercise has been used to treat depression! (I ask many of my clients to start walking daily, if they are not already doing so.) As exercise is so vital for our health and well-being mentally and physically (and spiritually), we benefit by creating a timetable for exercise in our life. If we do what we enjoy, then exercise will occur more frequently. I believe it's important for our mood, health and weight to exercise for thirty minutes every day. This can be as simple as a thirty minute brisk walk daily. If you have your doctor's approval, and you are physically fit enough, add strength training, such as yoga, pilates, fit ball or weight lifting, to further increase your fitness, stamina and improve your mental health. And I highly recommend everyone engages a personal trainer at some stage of his or her life, just to understand some of the techniques to exercising properly.

Have Constant Energy and Live Longer

Have you ever felt as though your body was just exhausted, that you just wanted to lie on the floor? Our bodies work really hard to support us. So how can we support our body in return? One way is by spending time sitting in the sun, just letting the rays fall on our skin. We can support our body by taking a deep breath—ahhh arrrr. We can support our body by being grateful, by sending beautiful energy, by telling our body, "Thank you! Thank you, breath; thank you, body!" We can support our body by exercising, keeping it fit and healthy, by doing yoga or Pilates, which work with the energy flow in our body. We can support our body by eating nutritious foods, including a healthy breakfast, sleeping eight or more hours per night, not being too overweight or underweight, drinking alcohol in moderation, and not smoking. Ensuring that we lead a happy life will also add to our longevity. *So help your body support you!*

Your Body Listens to Your Mind

Your thoughts create your health and your illnesses. Louise Hay, author of *The Power Is within You*, healed herself of cancer and has worked with many people who were sick and suffering from AIDS. During this time Louise noticed recurring patterns—the connection between the thought patterns and illnesses in the body.

Louise Hay created a dictionary of illnesses in her must-have book, *You Can Heal Your Life*. This book also includes the corresponding thought patterns and helpful affirmations to help you reverse these multitudes of illnesses from cancer to the common cold.

Whenever I have a tickle in my throat, an elevated temperature—any physical ailment—I check Louise's book to find the reason. Knowing there is a connection between the mind and body is extremely helpful. When we identify and stop the contributing unhelpful thoughts and replace these with helpful, tailor-made affirmations, we are well on our way to recovery. We need to identify conscious or subconscious thoughts and feelings, as these are contributing to our health or our sickness. I have experienced the healing power of this book, time and time again, for more than a decade.

Naturally, whenever I hear anyone say, "Oh, I think I am coming down with a cold," I cringe! So many people do not realize that their thoughts create their health, and many people make themselves sick. It takes a conscious effort to constantly monitor our thoughts and words. When you do, you cannot help but notice others using poor self-talk. What we believe creates our health and our future. We are affirming our reality with every thought. Imagine the reality we affirm when we say these things: "I can't give up smoking. My body is weak. I have low immunity. I always get tired in the afternoons. I always crave unhealthy food. Life is so hard. My memory is like a sieve. I just can't lose weight. Everything I eat goes straight to my thighs. I always get colds in winter. I feel so old. I will never be fit again. It doesn't matter what I do, if there is a cold around, I'll catch it."

When Your Body Fights You

When we feel in control of our destiny, when we eat well, exercise, and do what we love, our body normally supports us. In contrast, often in our busy life, our body does fight back. Sometimes we are too harsh; sometimes we rush too much, push ourselves too hard, and worry too much, filling ourselves with negative emotions. We don't give enough thought to the body that houses our spirit.

Sometimes we think about our body, but we think negative things—and our body fights back with sickness or we start having pain in our back or neck, our blood sugar can destabilize, we can put on weight, lose weight, have problems with our intestines, our hormones. We can accumulate toxins and suffer from regular headaches. It's really important for us to be connected to our body and to recognize the early signs of stress, fatigue, and illness. Some people are so "in their minds," so in their thoughts and emotions, so busy that they are out of tune with their body, like a soul disconnection. When they get sick, they complain. They feel as though their body is attacking them. They don't give a thought to all the negativity they are putting into their mind and body. They blame their body.

I am in tune with my body. And by being in tune, *I rarely get sick*. It's a large statement but I say it with confidence because if I do feel the start of something, like I may be fighting a virus, I take my body to bed. I take the day and night off if I can manage it. So it's take-away dinner for the family and it's in bed for me. I give my body a chance to fight by resting at the first sign of illness. I don't wait until I'm feeling really unwell. That was the way I lived before, but not now. As soon as I notice that feeling—flushed face, sore muscles, maybe just the start of a sore throat—it's off to bed and it's rest time. Then I think positive thoughts. I say to myself, "My body is fighting a bug and I am getting better," and I have full expectations to wake up the next day feeling better. And I usually do!

Is Addiction Ruining Your Life?

Those with serious addictions, such as alcohol or drugs, live a life full of extremes. A person who has an addiction lives with a dark cloud over their head, full of unresolved emotions. They turn to the addiction instead of facing their emotions and life's challenges. They often enter a world of guilt and self-pity, feel like victims, have anger issues, and unresolved emotions; it's a highly chaotic lifestyle. Smoking recreational drugs such as marijuana, taking "party drugs" on weekends, or drinking alcohol to excess can invite negative energy and events unknowingly into your life, or worse, can even rob you of your life. Release yourself to life fully by giving up self-defeating addictions. Whether it is an addiction to anger, drugs, smoking, alcohol, prescription painkillers, gambling, or food, addictions can cause disconnection from self, particularly from inner self, from friends, and from life.

Jill, a mother of three, began drinking a glass of wine daily after work in an attempt to escape the financial pressures and stress of being a solo mother. Her one or two glasses a night rapidly escalated to a bottle, and then the bottle became more than a bottle a day. Her ability to make rational decisions declined. She would put her children in the car and drive while intoxicated to buy more alcohol. Her entire life revolved around drinking—not to socialize but to numb her pain and try to escape her reality. Her emotions were mostly negative, and she lived with constant guilt, anger, self-hatred, and fear. So she would drink more. She was consumed daily by a constant need to get drunk. Eventually she lost custody of her children. She lost her home, her car, everything she owned, and she was left with nothing but the alcohol.

Fortunately, Jill eventually went to detox, rehabilitation, and her life is now on track. To maintain sobriety, Jill attends Alcoholics Anonymous meetings, and she uses mental strategies, boundaries, and cognitive behaviour therapy to keep her strong. Jill visualizes a wall between her and alcohol. On that wall are the faces of her new spouse and her children, who she is in contact with again. If she ever drinks alcohol again, Jill believes that wall will come crashing down, and her life will become hell again. This visualized wall is powerful, for it keeps Jill in a world where she is powerful and in control, and not the alcohol.

From my studies and from speaking with clients who have experienced alcohol-related issues, I believe people who drink alcohol usually fit into one of these four categories:

1. *Social Drinkers* enjoys a drink or two of alcohol while socializing, to relax and enjoy a night out with friends. If you asked the partner of a person who drinks socially, "Do you think your partner has a drinking problem?" the answer would normally be no. If you put alcohol or a soft drink in front of them and the drinks tasted the same, they would happily drink the soft drink. They drink for the taste and do not normally drink alone. The social drinker usually does not experience a negative mood change while drinking alcohol.

2. *Binge Drinkers* may drink alcohol once during the week, such as at a party or while out on the weekend; However, they consume large quantities of alcohol over a short period of time. Their motivation may be to show off around friends, attempt to gain confidence, or try to escape negative emotions. This binge drinking is very unhealthy for the body, and dangerous, as high alcohol in the blood reduces brain activity, hindering decision-making abilities. This often leads to actions that this person regrets, which can lead to reduced self-confidence and/ or self-esteem, and heightened sense of helplessness. Binge drinking can lead to dangerous blood alcohol levels, causing depression of the central nervous system and unconsciousness, and "sleeping it off" can lead to silent regurgitation and death. Binge drinkers may not view themselves as having drinking issues as they do not usually drink daily. However, the impact on the binge drinker's life is often detrimental.

3. *Emotionally Addicted Drinkers* drink alcohol in an attempt to numb their emotions, to escape reality or their guilt. They usually feel unhappy about themselves, their lives, or an aspect of their lives. They may have low self-esteem, anger, and they may have experienced trauma, abuse, or loss as a child or adult. They often have a lot of unresolved negative emotions— drinking alcohol only temporarily "hides" negativity, so life usually becomes worse when they are sober, as issues are not resolved. Angry outbursts, or unusual nastiness may occur frequently while the emotionally addicted drinker is intoxicated. They may or may not drink daily, but it's not about the quantity, it is their reason for drinking and the effect it has on them. These people may go to the bottle shop on the way home from a stressful day at work, or drink to feel relaxed and forget their issues.

4. *Chemically Addicted Drinkers* are chemically and physically addicted to alcohol. They often begin as emotionally addicted (see above) and then progress to physically (chemically) addicted, as their body becomes accustomed to drinking alcohol on a regular basis. They drink daily; it forms an integral part of their daily life. Most of their activities incorporate drinking, and many of their friends drink a lot. They usually experience issues related to priority management, relationships, and work. They may make poor decisions, have unresolved anger issues, and suffer poor health. They would have great difficulty not drinking for twenty-four hours. In some cases, the chemically dependent drinker will need to detox before rehabilitation to ensure they can safely reduce the alcohol in their body, as they are so highly dependent.

If alcohol or drugs are causing problems in your life, or if you are negatively affected by someone else's drinking, drug-taking, or addictions, please seek help from a counsellor, your local drug and alcohol government support service, Alcoholics Anonymous, Al-Anon, Alateen, or Narcotics Anonymous, to name a few. Visit www.aa.org, www.al-anon.org or www.na.org.

Stress in the Body

Author John Randolph Price, in his book *The Superbeings,* states tension and stress may lead to colds, constipation, headache, high blood pressure, and more. Our bodies reflect the mind. You may be overworked, overstressed, sending many negative messages out from your brain, leaving your body in turmoil. Some people live this stressed-out, over-adrenalized existence daily.

We all have stress. Stress is pressure, both mentally and physiologically. Often the pressure is external and related to life events, and many times it relates to pressure we put ourselves under. Stress can be the result of any factor from the following five areas:

1. *Perception:* perceived lack of time, feeling overwhelmed or over-committed, worrying about money and the future;
2. *Life Changes:* moving house, changing jobs, midlife crisis, retiring, aging;
3. *Relationship Issues:* having a child, separation, divorce, starting again with a new spouse, leaving home, conflict in the family with children or spouse, issues at school or work;
4. *Health:* being unhealthy, having illness or a disease, not having enough time to rest;
5. *Trauma:* death of friend or family member, grief and loss, accident.

Part of dealing with stress is avoiding the situations that make you feel stressed. We can also learn to live life in "this moment" or "just these next three hours" to avoid excessive worry. When we become present and work toward acceptance; when we learn to be assertive and have time to relax factored into our daily schedules, stress becomes easier to manage and less prevalent in our lives. When we put everything out of our mind and have faith that everything is working out for our best, life will become easier. Naturally, if we are stressed due to a loss of a loved one, we still need to take time out, be present, kind to ourselves, and patiently work through the stages of grief and acknowledge that time will help us heal.

Fatigue from Boredom

Have you ever woken up, had a shower, yet felt so drained that you found it almost impossible to dress and prepare for work? What about having a big day ahead, whether it is cleaning the house or doing mountains of washing or mowing the lawn, and you felt like your body was exhausted before you even started?

When fatigue overwhelms you, stop and think about what you are doing. Author Louise Hay states the underlying cause of fatigue is resistance and boredom. What is so terribly boring? Can you change what you are doing at that moment? If not, keep the end result in mind. If you are working at a job that makes you feel constantly fatigued, you may need to evaluate whether you should change jobs. Alternatively, if your regular daily activities make you feel drained, brighten up your routine. We all benefit by being excited about life, and not wasting precious time being bored. If being bored for only an hour or two can lead to fatigue, imagine what being bored for weeks (or years) could do to a person's body. If you are excited about your work, your relationships and your life, you are less likely to feel fatigued. *Avoid fatigue by doing what you love!*

Keep Your Body Energized Using Natural Remedies

The Chinese discuss a concept called *chi* (qi), the flow of energy. They talk about energy in our body being stuck and how we need to release this energy. Massage, acupuncture, and kinesiology all incorporate pressure points and work with releasing and moving energy around our body, to promote improved health and state of mind. More specifically, kinesiology works with Chinese acupuncture meridians and aims to balance energies, using muscle testing, while also incorporating knowledge of physiology and anatomy. The aim is to treat the person as a whole and restore balance. All these natural practices, including naturopathy, can be extremely helpful in gently guiding our energies through our bodies, restoring much needed balance, resulting in an improved sense of well-being, health, and energy.

As we are all unique, different methods will work best for each of us. Like any therapy, the proof is in the healing. If you are feeling stressed, jealous, anxious, depressed, overwhelmed, ill, or confused, seek help from a therapist, and in addition, consider working with a natural practitioner to achieve mind/body balance.

Food for Thought

The diet problem—I, like many women, have spent a lifetime trying almost every diet known to woman. Recently I met a very attractive woman in her late thirties with an amazing figure. She told me she *never* diets or goes to the gym! What! How could this be? Surely she must starve herself and live on carrot sticks to look as amazing as she does. No, instead, this woman said, "Oh, I eat cheese and crackers in the afternoon if I feel like it. I love chocolate and I eat it every day." What! To meet a human being who simply eats when she is hungry? She doesn't measure food or weigh herself every day. She doesn't count calories, obsess about the food she is going to eat, or feel guilty about the food she has eaten. She doesn't stare at the mirror and feel disgust. She said she doesn't hide in her bedroom and eat (like some other women I have spoken to). This woman simply eats when hungry, stops eating when she is satisfied, and has a healthy self-image.

What did this woman have that I did not? Different thinking when it comes to food! I have since met other women who have a healthy attitude toward food and dieting. They simply eat what they feel like, when they feel like it. Why do these women succeed? What are their secrets? Well, I asked them, and following are their guidelines for living diet free and looking fabulous:

1. Have a positive and kind self-image. Do not stand in front of the mirror throwing insult after insult at your reflection.

2. Understand why you eat—for health, to nourish your body, and give it energy.
3. Rarely eat between meals, or snack on fruit when you do.
4. Do not obsess about food or about the next meal.
5. Do not starve yourself.
6. Never binge eat!
7. Never deprive yourself. If you occasionally feel like having a piece of cake, have one.
8. Have chocolate in the home, and trust yourself to eat one or two pieces and not the whole block.
9. Eat mostly healthy foods, such as fruit, vegetables, and whole grains, etc.
10. Drink water. Only drink alcohol and soft drinks in moderation.
11. Exercise as a regular part of your lifestyle.
12. Do not eat for boredom, stress, or as an emotional response. Eat only when you are hungry.
13. Do not eat if you are not hungry. You do not have to eat at 12:30 p.m. just because it's lunchtime.
14. Do not eat everything on your plate just to be polite.

Give Your Body Some "Blob Time"

We all need "blob time." Time to sit or lie in front of the TV, read a magazine, stay in our pyjamas, and not wear makeup (or not shave for men), not even brush our hair or teeth if we don't want to. Blob time is downtime, times when we are not rushing around but simply doing what we want to do, and most importantly, resting physically and mentally. Try to do all the supermarket shopping, washing, cleaning, and exercise on weekdays in order to keep weekends free for rest, relaxation, and fun.

Homework—Are You Listening to Your Body?

1. Focus on your body throughout the day. How does it feel? Does it feel tired, stressed, angry, depleted, or in pain? These messages are best listened to and then interpreted.
2. Be grateful to your body and thank your body regularly for supporting you through everything.
3. When you talk about your body, listen to the words you use. Are they kind?

4. Your thoughts are powerful and can make you sick. If you feel the symptoms of a cold, what kind of things can you say to yourself to improve the situation?

5. What stressful events have you been through over the last twelve months? How does your body help you cope with stress in the short term? What strategies, both physical and mental, can you use to cope better with stress?

6. Do you have enough "blob time" in your life?

If a person would turn within and seek the light, the barrier would in time break away. Intuitive powers would develop, strange and wonderful thoughts would enter consciousness, and finally, the voice of wisdom within would be heard as the individual puts on a new man.—John Randolph Price

The messengers of intuition: nagging feelings, persistent thoughts, humour, wonder, anxiety, curiosity, hunches, gut feelings, doubt, hesitation, suspicion, apprehension, and fear.—Gavin De Becker

CHAPTER 5

ARE YOU LISTENING TO YOUR INSTINCTS?

You Have a Pre-Life Purpose

According to Mitchell Coombes, author of *Sensing Spirit*, before you came to this earth, before you were born, you decided what you wanted to achieve in this lifetime. You decided what tools you would need, what experiences you would need, and what impact you could make on this world. This is called the blueprint of your soul. When you grow up, you usually don't remember what you wanted to achieve in this lifetime. For this reason you were given a tool—your gut instinct, intuition, or higher self, as many call it.

This intuition is what keeps each of us on track. When you feel like everything is wrong in your life, it most probably is. When you feel like you are heading in the wrong direction, and you feel like screaming, or like you're being suffocated, then maybe everything is wrong. Stop and be led by how you feel, regardless of how ridiculous it seems. There are many schools of thought on a pre-planned existence. Whether this is correct or not, it certainly feels right and keeps me focused on my passions.

Create Your Heaven on Earth

Heaven or hell is here on earth; you do not have to wait until you die. We are the creators of our reality. We influence, observe, and create our own world. Even our perception of our life directly impacts our experiences. I believe we can create our own heaven on earth. You are creating your heaven (or hell) on earth with every thought, image, word, conversation, dream, goal, and action.

What is heaven on earth to you? Is it a fantastic romance, filled with passion and adventure? Is it a fashionable apartment in the city, or a country retreat, where you wake to the sound of birds? Is it living with your family in harmony, and regularly entertaining close friends? Does your heaven on earth include great wealth or simply no debt, or do you wish to escape the hustle and bustle of life and spend your afternoons digging in your organic vegetable garden? Do you want to work three days a week and have more time for you? Do you want to travel Europe, backpack across Australia, or go camping with the family? This is your life! You are the author in your life. Your life is meant to be a joy-filled adventure. It is not meant to be work, struggle, eat, sleep, pay bills, work, struggle … you are constantly creating with every moment. The more positive thoughts, conversations, images, and expectations, the more positive results, experiences, and moments you are likely to have. Fear, negativity, criticism, being angry, being unbalanced emotionally—these things will keep your heaven on earth at bay; they will rob you of your peace and steer you in a direction filled with disharmony, instead of clarity of mind, beauty, and joy.

Your life is like this: You are sitting at an exclusive restaurant, ordering your meal—except your meal is *your* life! Some people sit at this restaurant and complain, sulk, expect poor food, bad service, and some don't even order, so that is the life they get—filled with bad experiences. I want you to sit at this restaurant of life, relax, have a sip of water, forget everything that is going on in your life, and really imagine the life you want. Be decisive and clear. Order your meal (your heaven on earth) and then wait patiently and expect the waiter (the universe) to deliver what you ordered (or close to it). You cannot order from this waiter if you are fighting with a loved one, filled with self-pity, or distracted by negative emotions. Once you have ordered, have patience and faith that good things do come to those who wait—but only *if* you order them!

To have what you want in life, you need to spend time thinking of how you want your relationships, finances, home, work, hobbies, body, etc. to look and be. Brainstorm, discuss, research, put your focus on what you want, not on what you don't want. Be specific in your universe order. What do you want, exactly, in all the areas in your life? What would heaven on earth be to you? What can you do, day by day, that will lead you toward a more joy-filled, extraordinary existence? The universe will lead you to the possibilities, show you the way, and take care of all the small details. However, you need to put your order in first! Your thoughts are so powerful; fantasize and keep your eye on the prize! "Taste" the results as if they have already happened. Expect your plans to eventuate, stay focused, stay positive, be patient, and then, once the universe delivers your heaven on earth, enjoy—and say thank you.

The Power of an Aura

Have you ever walked into a room and felt like you could "cut the air with a knife" after an argument between two people? Have you ever felt physically weak or frightened as a result of someone else's anger; as if a hostile energy filled the room? Have you ever been near a stranger, and without him or her having spoken a word, you experienced a weird vibe that almost said "stay away"? Have you ever had a heated argument with your spouse that ended in silence? Then, as the other person silently moved through the house, you felt strong sadness, anger, or emotional intensity seemingly resonating from his or her body? Or have you ever felt relaxed and somehow comforted when meeting a new neighbour; as though you had known him or her your entire life? Have you noticed the way you can instantly feel happy and exhilarated when you are reunited with friends or family?

We humans are like radio transmitters, constantly giving out and picking up energy and signals. Our thoughts and emotions project outward while we simultaneously pick up the thoughts and emotions of others. Many experts agree that our words only make up approximately 7 percent of our communication, and the rest is made up of vocal tone and nonverbal communication. Our bodies "let out" how we feel, what we think, our opinions. Sometimes this is subtle, and sometimes it is not. Our auras (energy) give away so much! So when you feel a certain way about someone, you may simply be picking up messages from that person's energy. Most people can't see the energy in the aura, yet we can feel it; it is a great tool for sensing the moods and possibly anticipating reactions from others. How you "feel" about someone is usually a good indicator, as whatever is not being said is often being communicated through his or her aura.

We all have the ability to be psychic, to a small or large degree. Some people are avid believers in the paranormal, the strange and wonderful feelings they experience, and others only believe what they see. It is helpful and practical to be aware that we can often "feel" other people's energy, and it can be helpful for anticipating a person's actions. Auras are small and large, depending on the person. People emit good or bad auras, depending on how they are feeling and who they are. After spending time with someone (or with a group of people at a work conference, seminar, etc.), you may be left feeling flustered or not grounded, with thoughts seemingly racing around your mind. In this situation you may find it helpful to have a shower and cleanse your aura.

We humans pretty much wear our emotions on our sleeves as they flow outside our bodies, so others may feel what we are feeling. If you feel uneasy in a person's company, trust this feeling. Our bodies, our minds, are registering much more than what we can see.

The Power of Our Chakras

A chakra is an area in the body that collects energy. This subtle energy field is connected to our major organs, and it is believed that if our chakras become blocked, we can become sick and our emotions can become unbalanced. Many practices, such as yoga, acupuncture, massage, kinesiology, Reiki, and feng shui use this flow of chi (energy) around the chakras to promote better mental health and physical well-being.

There are seven chakras in our body, from bottom to top: root, sacral, solar plexus, heart, throat, third eye, and crown. According to the principles of chi (Chinese word meaning life force energy, also called ki, qi, or Prana) emotional issues, from sexual, financial, self-esteem, confidence, peace, creativity, assertiveness, wisdom, intuition, and much more are affected by the chakras and the flow of energy.

Healing unbalanced energy is so powerful, particularly if you are suffering from any emotional imbalance. Also, as everything in life is energy, it makes sense that when we detect an angry person's aura (an atmosphere, an electromagnetic field surrounding a person's body), we collect their energy/anger through our chakra and feel it intensely in our body. We are always giving out and picking up energy, so we need to be mindful of this.

Occasions Mark the Walls

Traumatic events can take place in some dwellings, and these events seem to scar those areas. Have you ever noticed when you have walked into a place where there has been a lot of animosity or sadness that you can feel uncomfortable in the room? Some houses have negative energy. It really doesn't matter what the house looks like, it's the energy inside that counts.

Keith bought a beautiful big house. He moved in with his family, and within a couple of months he was seeing a counsellor; he felt like he was having a nervous breakdown. He had always been so confident in his life and felt secure, yet the house seemed to change him. When his friends visited, they talked about a cold feeling. Keith and his wife had their nice furniture in the house, and it was such a lovely design, but it just seemed that there was no love in the house, only emptiness. He never felt like it was home, and neither did his wife. They eventually sold the house, moved on, and were much happier.

I could not live with that energy either, but many people are not as sensitive to the energy of their surroundings as much as others. We need to be aware of the energy we may pick up at different places, as experiences mark the walls and the energy is left behind. This energy can affect our lives, so be careful when picking your next home.

The Power of a Crowd

As an "audience member," you often feel "as one" on some deeply spiritual level with all the other audience members. Your moods and emotions can be easily swayed by the majority. This makes crowds a mighty force, or a possible risk, depending on the situation. There is a very real feeling when we are in a large group that we act as one.

Our thoughts, emotions, and energy, whether good or bad, radiates from us. This energy affects all those around us. As we are all energy, it is not surprising to know that experts often single out one person to reduce potential trouble. A friend of mine, who runs a nightclub, says everyone will be happy, drinking peacefully, and just one unhappy, nasty drunk person is enough to spoil the mood in the place. She says there are happy drunks and there are troublemakers—their energy affects the mood. Just one person can spoil the atmosphere. Similarly, an experienced dog trainer often removes a dog from his pack if the dog does not have the "right energy," as a dog with the wrong energy will negatively affect the pack. Dogs pick up on these energies instinctively, as do we. This confirms how powerful, psychic, and perceptive we humans truly are.

Our Need to Belong

Belonging is the human need to be accepted as a member of a group. Being part of certain groups can be good for your self-image, your self-esteem, and can make your feel emotionally stronger. When we connect, share experiences, and relate to others as part of a group, we can feel an increased sense of belonging and a heightened connectedness to humanity.

We are all part of a group, whether it be human beings, men, women, our family, our school, our workplace, our suburb, our political preferences, a sporting club, a social club—even our friendships form a group we belong to. We can also belong to a group temporarily, such as a group in the cinema, or a crowd at a football match or concert. In these groups the shared interest, passion, and proximity can contribute to a powerful sense of collected energy, which can increase emotions and intensity of these experiences. This may explain why a movie or football match seems more exciting when watched with others. This sense of unity that forms part of a group may work with you or against you.

As the common denominator is shared goals and pursuits, some groups are antisocial and members may have shared goals that are illegal or negatively impact their lives. Once again, if you do not feel right as part of a particular group, then you need to listen to your inner voice. Groups and crowds have the power to move us in a powerful and productive way, or in a negative direction. The shared energy, passion, and direction of a positive group can be a mighty force in your life and for this world.

Your Dreams and Nightmares Talk to You

Dreams and nightmares are fascinating. They touch us, inspire us, and scare us, yet they are a vital part of understanding who we are. Dreams can show us areas in our lives we can improve or highlight areas we may have overlooked, and our nightmares can warn us off catastrophes ahead. Feel free to use these four basic theories to help decode your dreams and nightmares:

1. *Dreams contain messages from the unconscious:* According to Sigmund Freud, a dream is a "wish fulfilment." Our unconscious stores information, usually a conflict we are not aware of, and it stores this information in a basic, usually disturbing, form. The preconscious, in its relaxed state during sleep, allows this image to come through. This image/symbol may need to be translated.

    Mark had spent years fighting in the courts due to a painful divorce that left him with minimal access to his son. Mark often dreamt he was in his marital home with his childhood sweetheart, Pamela, once again. There was no divorce, no custody battle, and he was happily married again, as if time had been reversed. In some way, could Mark be wishing for this to be the case? Deep in his unconscious, perhaps he wishes he had never divorced? Or was his mind simply reviewing his traumas while he slept and working toward reconciling the events?

2. *Dreams contain messages from the self (personality/emotions):* According to Fritz Perls, co-founder of gestalt therapy, our dreams represent rejected, disowned parts of the self, unexpressed emotions and unfinished situations. He indicated that all characters and objects in our dreams represent parts of the self. When we act out each of these parts in real life, we can gain a greater understanding of elements of our self that we may have disowned. Fritz Perls viewed dreams as a way of accessing the unconscious. We may also discover feelings we have not acknowledged; feelings we may have overlooked, and some of these may need to be worked through with a counsellor or psychologist, as they may be traumatic.

3. *Dreams contain messages from our higher self (our soul):* Our dreams often show us messages from our higher self, and warn us. This may be a symbol, which we know terrifies us. For example, if you dream about large spiders, there may be something scary in your life that you are overlooking. Our higher self is always trying to communicate with us, and this can be done with dreams. We can learn more about our self, our motivations, fears, and goals by looking closely at our dreams. When I dreamt I was getting an axe to kill a large snake that had wrapped itself around my son, I knew in that moment I instinctively want to protect him. When he was about to leave for his first camping trip with friends, I ensured he had packed all necessities.

4. *Dreams contain messages from the spirits:* Sometimes we have visitors in our dreams. This may be a person who is alive, or someone who has died. These dreams are very vivid and can be scary, yet the messages are often clear. I have spoken to many clients who have told me about being visited by their loved ones who have passed away. Many dreams contain warnings and important information.

Recently, Lara woke and warned her husband (who works for the water police) of a lost boat, and described the flora around the boat. Her husband called her from work and asked her to describe the vegetation around the missing boat, as a hired boat full of people had not returned to dock. She described the vegetation and he found the missing boat, which was on the other side of an island. Lara is not a paid psychic, she is a nurse. Lara trusts her gut instinct, believes in premonitions, and pays attention to her dreams.

Your Soul Is in School

In life, we go through stages of achievement physically, intellectually, emotionally, developmentally, and spiritually. We may go through levels in our employment and win promotions at work as we become more skilled. Developmentally, we go through many stages where our needs change physically, socially, and physiologically as we change. And life also has levels, but these levels are not often talked about. These levels relate to our evolving as spirits—as human beings. The more we learn, the higher we evolve. Life is constantly giving us lessons! The lessons are not work-related or study-related, they are life-related. Some of these lessons are extremely difficult. We benefit when we evolve and learn from these, and, in many cases, when we help others and make the world a better place through our lessons of pain.

Some cultures believe our soul evolution in this life makes a large impact on our next life, after reincarnation. The more we know about how life works, the rules, darkness, light, how the universe works, the more success we will have in this, and possibly future, lifetimes. I hope this book helps you understand more about the complexities of our life, so you can evolve faster, and make this—your journey—so profoundly more enjoyable.

When we learn life's lessons and spiritually evolve, life becomes less complicated, as if we have "seen the light." We understand more about how to live a more fulfilling existence, achieve our goals, and know (and receive) what we want from life.

Miracles and Blessings Multiply

I believe in appreciating all the miracles in our lives, small to large. Have faith in miracles and watch out for them in your life. Every child is a miracle. Every near-death experience is a miracle. Every healing is a miracle. I see miracles constantly, often in my counselling rooms.

Everyone experiences miracles, but some people don't name them and instead say, "Whoa, that was lucky!" Miracles are very much like coincidences; they happen a lot, and the more we acknowledge them, the more we have them in our lives. A miracle in your life may be an astounding event, such as the conception or birth of your child, meeting your soul mate, or a fast or profound physical or emotional healing. Your miracle or blessing may be a near-death experience, a healing of an addiction, receiving extra money just in time to pay the bills, an unexpected new work opportunity, a new friendship, or successfully avoiding a collision on the highway. Then there are also smaller blessings, the ones that happen every single day. Today, some of your blessings may simply be bringing the washing in before it rains, remembering to do your son's reading before school, a quiet day at work so you can clean your desk and schedule upcoming appointments in your diary, the weather changing from hot to cool, or enjoying a movie with your partner in the evening.

The more we focus on our miracles and blessings, the more we experience. And the more we experience, the happier our lives become. Isn't this beautiful and divine? What we focus on expands ... so focus on miracles and blessings; all the wonders in life from the large to the small are all worth acknowledging and being grateful for.

Everything Is Energy—Be Calm in a Crisis

Ever tripped over or fallen off a bicycle? Did you notice how time seemed to slow down as you were falling? Similarly, in a crisis, or life threatening situation, our bodies are designed to help us. Our bodies change into "fight or flight" mode, our adrenalin increases, our heart races, blood flows quickly, breathing comes faster ... and it feels like our bodies have sped up. We are more alert, we can think and act faster than normal, and life seems to be in "slow motion." In a crisis, we need to be calm and present, and we need to accept the situation in order to act decisively. Our full attention and focus are needed, so we cannot afford to be distracted by thoughts such as, *This can't be happening to me. Why is this happening? Who is responsible?* We can perform best in a crisis by simply "being," thinking everything through, one idea at a time, staying calm, being in the moment, remaining positive, and leaving all the emotional negativity for another time. Surrender to this moment and take action.

Jane had been out with friends. When she arrived home, she heard screams from upstairs. She found her teenage son, Josh, unconscious, surrounded by confused, drunk, and scared friends. Josh had been drinking with his friends, and as Jane looked at the floor at her unconscious son, who was covered in vomit and not breathing, she felt angry and terrified. Jane prioritized. She instructed one of the friends to call an ambulance. She ensured Josh was in the recovery position, that his airway was clear and he was breathing again. Jane sensed that Josh needed more than first aid. She felt, on some level, that Josh was struggling to live, that he was somehow "not in his body," as if his spirit were in the room. She also sensed he was saying, "I'm sorry. Good-bye." Jane felt that, most importantly of all in this moment, she needed to be pure energy—*pure love*. In this delicate life or death state, her son needed every ounce of positive energy around him. Jane told herself she would only think positive thoughts and deal with her anger and fear later.

The ambulance arrived, and Josh was rushed to hospital for treatment. When Josh recovered, Jane asked him what he had felt during this incident, and he said, "I thought I was dying. I heard my friends saying, 'He's not breathing.' I was fighting really hard to get control of my body." Jane had been right. In those critical moments, Josh needed practical, lifesaving first aid, and he also needed every ounce of positive energy and love to survive.

Listen to the Screams of No from Within!

How can we protect ourselves from darkness? Anger can make people change. It can bring a negative element to the air. You can be in a situation that is safe one minute but need to evacuate the next! Bad things do happen to good people. Luckily there are many ways in which we are warned of upcoming events. There are coincidences, dreams, bad thoughts, reading someone's energy, and sometimes just plain logic. However, the most important tool we have for avoiding danger is our intuition (gut instinct). It works for us minute by minute, warning us.

How? Our brain is complex. While we are using a certain part of our brain, other parts work for us, registering potential dangers and then triggering a plethora of responses. These responses may be foreign to us, but they can save our lives. If we are parked outside our house, about to enter and suddenly feel terror we cannot explain, we need to understand that our eyes and mind could have worked together to notice the light on upstairs, an ex-boyfriend's car parked three houses away, and the gate slightly open. Our intuition could also be trying to warn us. (For more on fear and survival signals, please read *The Gift of Fear* by Gavin De Becker). Terror and/or over-worry, without logical reason, needs to be acknowledged, respected, and listened to. If you have an anxiety disorder or suffer from a lot of stress, then terror could simply be an emotional reaction to your current issues. However, if you do not have anxiety/worry issues and find yourself in a situation where you are terrified and can't shake the bad feelings— even worse if you have violent visuals running through your mind—be careful! Similarly, if you are in a place and feel the need to get out—leave immediately. Whether or not it is a party or a function, if the urge is intense, listen to it and safely exit. If you don't *feel* safe, you may not *be* safe even if everything seems okay.

In life we can stop, assess, and remove ourselves to safety if we hear *no, no* from within. In this way, we can work toward avoiding the violent or dangerous situations in life.

You Choose Your Parents

Many years ago I heard about reincarnation, about the concepts of us as human beings waiting as souls to come into our bodies, and part of this was choosing our parents. We apparently choose our parents so we can learn from them. Our parents can teach us so many things as they prepare us for our adult life. They teach us how to live, and how we *don't* want to live, and we can learn from their mistakes. We learn from how they act in the world. We learn by two distinct ways, consciously and unconsciously.

The way they live their lives models for us how we can live or don't want to live our lives. Think about your parents and your relationship with them. Do your parents have attributes you really like? Do you want to be like them? Do they have behaviours and mannerisms you'd like to consciously not copy?

Frequently I listen to my clients talk about their parents and their relationships. And even if they suffered verbal or physical abuse, clients often tell me they have learned from these experiences. They choose to live their lives very differently. Our parents help us in our journey by their example. What have your parents taught you about life? Are you listening to these lessons?

There Is Magic, Joy, and Power in Acceptance!

If we don't want to become stressed, if we don't want to use a lot of energy worrying and complaining, then we need to stop fighting against life. It is easy to look at what happens to us and then complain. Yet when we accept what is, then we have power to act. When we accept the current moment, we can have joy and peace. We benefit by going along with the flow of life, trusting the process, and when we experience hardship, trauma or losses, our eventual aim is acceptance.

The process may be a long and a challenging road, but acceptance is where we ultimately find peace. Acceptance is so magical; we cannot change and transform our lives, or ourselves, until we first accept who we are, what we have done, or where we might have slipped up. Complaining and blaming takes our power away. Acceptance puts us in the moment, and it is in this moment that we truly have power—the power to act and the power to make changes.

So if you are running late for an appointment, if schedules change, meetings are cancelled, or the venue you seek is unavailable, try to understand that life is far more intricate and complicated than we can possibly imagine. The universe may simply be conspiring in your benefit: to fulfil your deepest desires, teach you, or keep you safe. Sometimes life seems frustrating, yet when we step back and accept this moment and these obstacles, we allow life to unfold. We are part of a larger process of life, much bigger and more meaningful than we can possibly comprehend. By allowing the process to happen, by not fighting against life's apparent "obstacles," we allow ourselves to experience a much deeper level of peace and joy.

Homework—Are You Listening to Your Instincts?

1. Make a list of how you can you create your own heaven on earth (for example, look at your home, career, family, relationships, friendships, holidays, finances, habits, etc.). What does heaven on earth look like to you? The more you can paint this picture, the closer you are to living in your heaven on earth.

2. List the times in your life when you heard the screams of no from within. Did you listen? You can use this inner voice in every area of your life to achieve greater clarity, safety, improved decision making, and greater peace and happiness.

3. List all the groups you are part of. How do you feel when you participate in these groups? Do you feel strong? Do you feel accepted? Do you feel positive?

4. Are you listening to your dreams? They contain messages, information, warnings, and disowned parts of yourself. Dreams often need to be decoded; and when you understand the meanings, they can have a powerful impact on your life. Keep a dream diary and write your dreams down as soon as you wake.

5. List all the miracles and blessings you can recall. Every day, notice and be grateful for these.
6. In an emergency, keep your thoughts and energy positive, helping you to stay calm, enabling you to act fast, be in the moment, and do one thing at a time with increased focus.

We are all connected. We are entangled; if you want to call it quantum entanglement, fine. But we are entangled. And there is no real separation between us, so that what we do to another, we do to an aspect of our self.—William A. Tiller

Co-dependents become so preoccupied with others that they neglect their true self—who they really are. When we focus so much outside of ourselves we lose touch with what is inside of us: our beliefs, thoughts, feelings, decisions, choices, experiences, wants, needs, sensations, intuitions.—Charles L. Whitfield

CHAPTER 6

ARE YOU LISTENING TO YOUR RELATIONSHIPS?

Our Relationships with Family and Our Future Relationships

We are shaped by our relationships with family. We learn how to manage conflict by arguing with siblings, and we can be motivated to achieve great wealth in adulthood by experiencing childhood poverty. When people are dysfunctional, it often stems from their family relationships, as people behave the way they do in the context of their relationships. These relationships with our family members, and in many cases dysfunctional patterns, are ongoing and sustained by a constant series of actions and reactions between family members.

A family therapist may do a genogram (a diagram displaying the family relationships) to identify current and multigenerational emotional patterns, and patterns such as addiction and violence. By looking at our parents, we can see if there are any patterns of coping mechanisms (such as drinking after a stressful day)

123

or self-limiting beliefs (about self and life) that may have been copied subconsciously. Ideally in a family, members share tasks, talk openly, support each other, love each other, and communicate directly. Direct communication is the best form of communication.

In many cases however, dysfunctional patterns develop:

- *High-conflict relationships*: Two people argue a lot—they snap at each other, correct each other, and invest great energy in arguing daily.

- *Enmeshment/Fused:* Two people become over-involved in each other's lives; personal boundaries are unclear, often resulting in reduced competence, independence, and autonomy. This is very common in codependency, where someone worries excessively about another person's issues, life, and emotions.

- *Disengagement:* Two people are disconnected emotionally and know little about each other's lives and emotional needs. This can lead to low self-esteem, loneliness, or feelings of isolation. Some causes could be people who are workaholics, or have addictions or resentment.

- *Coalitions:* An alliance between two people, usually "isolating" or "ganging up" on another. This can form part of a triangulation, where a person is excluded and left on the outside.

- *Triangulation:* In systems theory (founded by psychiatrist and professor of psychiatry Murray Bowen), the focus is shifted to an outsider, usually in relationships with high anxiety or disconnection. For example, a mother may give most of her attention to her children, as she is increasingly dissatisfied with her spouse. A father may work a lot, due to emptiness in the marriage (making his work the outside "relationship").

- *Scapegoat:* In some families, one person is blamed for the entire family disharmony. This person may have a mental disorder, a syndrome (such as Asperger's), or drug and/or alcohol addiction, and all blame is directed his or her way.

Murray Bowen believes that when families are fused, or emotionally disconnected, independent decision making and self-growth are hindered. Ideally, a person can differentiate from his or her family and work toward a healthy balance between emotional connection and independence from his or her family, thereby fostering self-development, reduced anxiety, and increased happiness.

When I am working with a client I often ask about his or her childhood for the following reasons: to find out how healthy the relationship was between the client and the client's parents; to establish possible low self-esteem; to find out how good his or her role models were for coping with life and relationships; and to find out what possible issues the client may present with that are related to his or her childhood.

In family therapy, there are many aspects of a family that are important to learn about. Part of growing up and evolving is to look at our parents at some point in our lives, and identify what we feel they did that we can learn from and aspire to be like. We also look at what we can learn from our parents' behaviour that we would like to challenge, that we would like to stand apart from and possibly go in a different direction. This independence, this difference, this pulling away from family is really important as part of our growth.

Yet things can go wrong when people want to please their parents or even put their parents' wishes before their own spouse's. In these highly dependent relationships, people may hear a parent's voice in their head when they try to make decisions, important life decisions that may involve their own family, their own life, or their own relationships. If you hear the voices of your parents in your head, really decipher what you believe to be true for you, and what was true for them but does not resonate for you. It's your life. You will be fulfilled and happy when you make your own decisions based on how you feel, and not simply on trying to impress your parents.

You Are Your Friends

Our friends play a very significant role in our lives. They influence us, support us, entertain us, laugh with us, cry with us, and ultimately shape us. Some friends are only in our lives for a few years and others for a lifetime. Sometimes in life, gaining new friends can be like a breath of fresh air. Due to our continual spiritual and personal growth, making new friendships can be a beautiful way to encourage growth.

We are greatly influenced by those friends who we regularly spend time with. Accordingly, we need to choose our friends wisely because we learn from them subconsciously. We cannot help but be transformed (positively or negatively) by those we spend time with. We are chameleons. We are molecularly changed/altered by people we associate with. When we are with people, we breathe atoms in and out. Those atoms have been in these people—their energy, thoughts, experiences, attitudes, and behaviours. All these atoms affect us, and change us.

Think about your friends, the people you spend time with. Do you respect them? Do they possess the qualities you want to possess? Do you enjoy being with them? Do they make you feel alive, like a better person? Are you happy in their presence? Do they listen to you? Do they support you? Do you enjoy listening to and supporting them?

Friends are much more than just people you spend time with to have fun. Ideally they are people you aspire to be like, who possess skills and characteristics you admire. They are your teachers, whether you like it or not. Over time, day by day, you will become like those people—your friends.

Friends are the diamonds in what can often be an abrasive life. We are truly honoured to have great friends, punctuating our significant moments in life.

We Are Not Separate from Other Humans

We all hurt, watching others hurt. If there is a catastrophe on the other side of the world and we see it on television, we hurt. If we walk past a couple in the street fighting, or someone being abused, a young child being yelled at by their mother, we feel the pain. We feel emotional. We are all connected. Humanity is connected, so much so that if we praise others, we benefit by feeling better. If we criticize others, we suffer by feeling worse. You cannot do anything to anyone else without it affecting you. Everyone, in some way, is a reflection of our self. We can relate to other people because we either work with them, married them, gave birth to them, live with them, socialize with them, or we don't want to be like them! When we are annoyed by someone, often we share the same annoying habits as them—that is why they stand out and make us annoyed.

Our world (our relationships and humanity) is a reflection of *us*. When we realize that we all want the same thing on earth, that we are all on the same adventure called life then we realize that we are linked to our fellow human beings. Understand that to *love your neighbour as yourself* is really—to love your neighbour, is to love yourself. When we have any bitterness towards another, any disconnect, any resentment … we suffer. When we look at humanity with love and acceptance, understanding that we are all united, we are all humans wanting the same thing on the same journey—we will feel peace, love and joy.

Are You Controlling or Controlled?

We cannot control anyone else. They are not our puppets, regardless of whether they are our children or spouses. We can only control ourselves, and sometimes we struggle with this. We cannot control our destiny. We can only put out there what we want, have a positive expectation, put the effort in, but we cannot control the outcome. We need to be divorced from the outcome. We need to let destiny happen. We humans naturally want to control. We want to control so much in our lives, yet we only have complete control over ourselves and our emotions. Our happiness is not possible if we are trying to control everything in our lives, including people. When trying to control others we become frustrated and angry and feel rejected. In my counselling office, I often see couples where one person attempts to dominate the other. They are seeking counselling because they are unhappy, because this is not working. It is not good for the controlling person and it's not good for the controlled. It's a trap. It's an illusion.

If we want to have peace and joy daily, we need to resign ourselves—we can influence others in a positive way and set broader goals, and that's where our power really stops.

Do You Worry Too Much about Everyone Else?

If your mother or father had a drinking problem during your childhood, there is a very good chance you have "codependency." Codependency is where your boundaries aren't very clear. You care about everyone, but you try to help everyone, save everyone, look after everyone, and stop everyone from being hurt. Instead of caring for and focusing on yourself, you care for and worry obsessively about the lives of your family, even your friends and their opinions. (A part of codependency is indecision, as a person with codependency places more importance on the opinions of others over their own.) Codependency is a form of behaviour that one enters into in a relationship, which is maladjusted. And this behaviour, this way of being in the relationship, is normally modelled by a parent, or parents.

The most common modelling of this behaviour is when a parent has alcoholism, drug addiction, or a long-term illness. (It has been well documented that children of alcoholics often marry alcoholics—*so the codependency continues*.) People who have codependency have boundary issues and invest a lot of time and energy worrying about, thinking about, and trying to save or help family members or friends. In my counselling environment, when I am talking to couples, I like to put them in one of three categories: healthily independent, too independent, or codependent. In the first one, the husband and wife are happily living their own life and then meet together in the middle and share life. In the second example, ultra-independent, the couple live separate lives. They share a house, but there is little intimacy and the friendship is limited. There is distance and emotional disconnection. This is not a healthy way to be in a relationship. The third way is codependency, where one person worries excessively about the other, and quite often in this relationship alcohol seems to be an issue.

If you recognize codependency, you will benefit by reassessing your boundaries. Take little steps to detach somewhat from the dependency and to stop the excessive worrying and attachment, and work on changing your focus to yourself and your concerns. Once you have identified this pattern, you can make a conscious effort to change. According to author, physician, and psychotherapist, Charles L. Whitfield, in his book, *Co-dependence: Healing the Human Condition*, people with codependency have a tendency to look to others for happiness and avoid listening to their inner voice. They may put great efforts into looking elsewhere and not at themselves. This may lead to addictions, perfectionism, workaholism, or self-medicating, and more, while the codependent person continues on a journey of avoiding his or her *true self*. If you have codependency, seek help from a psychologist, counsellor, or family therapist.

Are You an "Energy Vampire"?

In our social interactions, while we are talking to each other and enjoying each other's company, we are actually exchanging energy, and there are ways we can be robbed of this energy. We can be left feeling depleted after spending time with someone I call an "energy vampire." This person may zap our energy in a variety of ways. One way is for them to tell us their hard-luck story, and when they do, everyone opens up and says, "Oh! That's terrible. You poor thing! That's so sad," and gives the energy vampire, who is playing the victim, their energy.

Another example of an energy vampire is someone who is sitting with a group of people and everyone is taking part in the conversation, and having a great time, and this person starts talking about an issue in his or her life. This vampire overtakes the conversation and doesn't seem to recognize (or care) that he or she has talked for a long time. This person has used up a lot of the group's time, and a lot of energy is focused on him or her.

There are people in the group who aren't getting a chance to talk. Life is not structured, and when you are in an informal situation you don't have turns as such, but there is an unwritten rule. When you are with groups of people, everyone who wants to talk has the chance. When people participate in group conversations, their energy levels rise and they feel great. It is only when an energy vampire comes along and wants to steal the show, and talk about his or her latest holiday, latest adventure, or latest drama that most of the time is consumed by listening to the energy vampire.

Do you know people like this? In a conversation with a variety of people, ideally everyone has an opportunity to have a chat, so everyone can feel enriched. We all need opportunities to share and contribute. In balanced conversations we often feel fulfilled. When conversations are out of balance, we may feel empty and frustrated.

Go Forward with Love

Have you ever worked with a person you found annoying? Have you ever gone to a new workplace and been told, "Whoa! Be careful of her—she is really nasty!" Ever had a relative, or someone else, make you feel inferior? When we are forced, whether it be by work or family relationships, to spend time with other people who make us feel uncomfortable, we can make a change in the dynamic.

I've had a couple of instances when I have known people and become negative and uncomfortable within their energy. I've had to soul search to try to find the answers to how to work these relationships so that it could be a win-win situation, a positive experience for us both. I really like most people I meet in this world. So when I come across someone I don't, I become perplexed. So I created a technique I call *go forward with love*. When I meet people who make me feel uncomfortable, when I greet them I become a ball of love. I smile, and it is not fake, it comes from the inside. I feel joyful and I celebrate this person. "Hi! How are you? You're looking fabulous today. Have a cuppa with me? Join me for a drink? So glad you are here." And do you know what? The relationships that were challenging, the people I had at the top of my most-annoying-list who *were* challenging—have fallen right off the list.

Going forward with love is a way for us to connect with these people, to take the negativity out of the relationship, and to be able to enjoy them. Previously I may have been wondering what this person thinks of me. What's going on? Now, instead of psychoanalyzing the relationship, I just go forward with love and the benefits are extraordinary.

If, however, going forward with love does not work, and you continually feel uncomfortable or attacked by a co-worker or relative, for example, then you may wish to take your power back! Depending on the situation, you can avoid them, confront them, or end the relationship by simply *letting them go* with love.

Relationship Therapy

I constantly meet with new couples facing challenges and we work together to achieve their goals of finding happiness again. Normally couples have issues due to a lack of strategy. For this reason, I wrote the book *Honeymooners Forever*. The steps in the book are as follows:

Step 1. Treat your partner like a lover, not a spouse.

Step 2. Be yourself and let your partner be himself or herself.

Step 3. Communicate well every day.

Step 4. Invest time and money in your relationship.

Step 5. Stop finding fault and start praising.

Step 6. Plan the romance.

Step 7. Restore the passion.

Step 8. Learn how to avoid or survive an affair.

Step 9. Children should enhance, not destroy, your marriage.

Step 10. Argue effectively.

Step 11. Improve your financial situation.

Step 12. Avoid and survive everything else life throws at you.

When counselling couples, I ask, "If I were to wave a magic wand over this relationship, and it would magically be transformed into the exact way you want it, how would this relationship be different to how it is today?" This forms the goal. Relationship therapy is often based on solution-focused therapy, where therapists and clients work toward a common goal and focus on the present and future, rather than on the past. (A relationship is very "in the moment," based on daily interactions and actions, and can change and improve rapidly if both parties work towards this change.) I then give the client homework tailor-made to their situation. However, I usually give the following tips for homework as well:

Honeymooners Forever Couples Homework

1. *Follow the strategy:* For the fastest and most dramatic change in your relationship, please read steps 1 and 5 and apply immediately. Once you apply step 1 and treat each other with

the respect, love, and courtesy with *every single* interaction, the relationship will quickly improve. Also, it is really important to change your mindset, and for this reason please read step 5 and stop criticizing your partner and begin praising him or her at every possible opportunity. Once you start praising instead of criticizing, you will see more good in your spouse.

2. *Thirty-minutes-a-day rule:* To be emotionally connected, you need to be constantly communicating, and not just about who is taking the rubbish out. You need a chance every day to relax, enjoy each other, and talk about your lives. These talks form the glue that keeps you connected. Without these chats you are simply roommates sharing a house, bills, and children. Feel free to use some of this time per day for your arguments. If you have long-standing resentments, the more you open up and discuss your feelings, the less resentment you will experience. Resentment is often caused by unexpressed hurt, anger and emotional disconnection. Resentment destroys passion and kills relationships. Help to keep resentment out of your relationship by using the thirty-minute rule.

3. *Are your priorities in order?* Where does your spouse rank in your priorities? Make a list of your life's priorities, and see how close to the top your spouse is. If your relationship is not close to the top, you will always put other activities before spending time with your spouse. Fall in love with your spouse again by making him or her a high priority and by giving your most precious resources—your time and love.

4. *Change your attitude:* To give this relationship the best chance, you need to be positive. If you are ready to transform your relationship and bring it back to its former glory, do not allow negative thoughts, such as separating, enter your mind. While you are working on this relationship and working on reconnecting, every ounce of your energy is required

for the healing to be completed. If you are second-guessing yourself, feeling as though you are wasting your time while simultaneously working on this relationship, you are like a bike rider trying to go backward and forward at the same time. Give yourself six months working with this program, and if you are not happy at the end of those six months, then you may wish to entertain another plan of action. Not every relationship is worth saving, but while you are working on yours give it all you have, which includes all your positive energy, positive visualizations, and positive mindset ... and don't let negativity creep in!

5. *Communicate well and be assertive:* It is vital to express your needs and feelings to your partner. Using the "I" stance, rather than "you" stance will be more easily accepted and less interpreted as an attack. For example, if you are feeling emotionally isolated, you could say, "I feel lonely. I miss you," rather than, "You always neglect me," which could come across as an accusation. You will also benefit by fine tuning your listening skills and learning to "blank" your mind and stop your constant internal dialogue, so that you can hear what your spouse is saying. If you are not free to listen at that moment, let him or her know, and make a time to talk later. Always be prepared to be present, listening and giving your full attention. In a relationship, you both need to have your needs met. This is only possible if both parties are assertive and discuss their needs, wants, and wishes. If you cannot discuss your needs, you will most likely become resentful, and resentful spouses usually lose interest in bedroom activities ... so the spiral of disconnection continues.

6. *Argue well:* One of the most important parts of being in a healthy, loving relationship is learning how to argue well. You may be lucky enough to have parents who are good role models,

or learned great conflict-management skills with your siblings or at work. Without these skills you will most likely become resentful, withdrawn, unsatisfied with your relationship, and emotionally disconnected. It is not how often you argue that counts (unless you are a high-conflict couple) but how you argue. I cannot emphasize enough how important it is to argue well. Ongoing anger, anger that is constantly pushed aside, will destroy a relationship. Resentment is healed when you talk about the issues during gentle arguments. Arguing over your resentments is like opening a wound, applying the antiseptic, and dressing it. Only then can the wounds heal! When you avoid arguing, this will kill your relationship, slowly, as the wounds fester and spread. So start arguing.

Argue more effectively with these five steps:

Step 1. Calm down: When you feel angry and nasty words are coming into your mind, this is the time to say to your spouse, "Time out," and then make a time to discuss these feelings later that night, before going to sleep, when you are both relaxed. If you sleep on anger, you will magnify these negative emotions, so you need to have the discussion before going to sleep if possible.

Step 2. Have a meeting ASAP: Treat your argument like a meeting. Conduct this meeting in a quiet area, with no distractions such as television, computers, or children. You both take turns being the speaker while the other listens. Do not interrupt each other. Begin sentences with *I statements* such as, "I need…" "I want…" or "I feel…," so you don't look as though you are accusing your spouse of anything. You own responsibility for your feelings. You may even wish to list topics and then make notes as you talk and listen.

Step 3. Be polite: Remain calm, treat each other with respect. Do not raise your voices and do not swear at each other. No name calling, abusive comments, personal attacks, silent treatments or storming off in anger. Avoid arguing under the influence of alcohol.

Step 4. Be thorough: Discuss issues, events and all associated feelings. In many cases, your spouse may just need to be listened to; he or she may simply need to discuss their frustrations. Discuss any unmet needs, unexpressed anger (resentments), fears, misinterpretations, or emotional pain. Ensure you both understand how the other is feeling. Ideally your are working towards collaboration but will settle for a compromise. Decide on a new direction, set new boundaries, and/or create an action plan.

Step 5. Get back to love: The goal of an argument is to resolve issues, reduce negativity in the relationship, and get back to love. Try to end the argument with positive energy by having increased quality time, enjoying a warm hug together, or having a date night. Spending quality time bonding after an argument should help you both become emotionally and physically intimate again. Having an argument is not all bad; it gives you the opportunity to re-connect after the argument. It is such a great opportunity to show love, empathy, teamwork and understanding for each other's feelings. Change the energy in your relationship from anger to love. It is more fun to love your spouse, than to be angry with them! If you do not express how you feel, you could remain angry.

Is Your Relationship Abusive?

In some relationships, one partner may control the other in a maladaptive, excessive, and dominating way. Often the spouse being controlled does not realize, until the relationship is over, that he or she lived in a cycle of control and abuse.

The following are some factors often seen in a cycle of control. Does your spouse do any of the following: threaten, intimidate or verbally, emotionally, or physically abuse you; isolate you from family or friends, blame you for his or her issues, and/or heavily restrict your finances?

The pattern of control is usually so similar from couple to couple who share this destructive trait that it is uncanny. Accordingly, when I speak with couples, I make sure I look out for this pattern of control or abuse. In this pattern, the partner who is abusive, the person who maintains most of the control is often successful, well-manicured, and polite (to those outside the relationship). In many cases, they are charming. The spouse who is being emotionally manipulated or abused often appears resentful, and in many cases, seems unhappy and does not appear to be coping well. In most cases the relationship begins normally, yet over time the controlling or abusive spouse begins to control or abuse more often. Small things first, and it escalates. In this pattern, the controlled spouse normally withdraws emotionally and often develops depression.

Author, Dr. Lenore Walker has written many books on domestic violence, including *The Battered Woman*, and is well known for developing the *cycle of abuse*, which shows four phases of abuse:

- tension building;
- incident;
- reconciliation;
- calm.

Because the abusive person is not always abusive and is often kind and loving (particularly in the reconciliation stage), a person may become confused as his or her partner is constantly flicking from one phase to another. As the abuse may not always be constant or the abused person may feel responsible for the abuse, the abused person feels hope that the situation will change, and is more likely to remain in the relationship. Also, because the controlling or abusive spouse has often isolated his or her partner from friends and family, the partner who is being controlled or abused does not get the opportunity to discuss the situation, gain outside perspectives, or receive support, making the situation more challenging, so often the control and abuse continues.

These issues are complex, and a person in these situations should seek professional help from an organization that specializes in abuse and from a counsellor, psychologist, or doctor. *Don't be a prisoner.* Not in your job or with your kids or in your marriage. In a happy relationship you will often feel some healthy boundaries; in an over-controlling or abusive relationship, you will often feel imprisoned and suffocated. Never let others rule your life. You should not be controlled or suffocated—it is a nightmare for the spirit, and in some cases, can be life threatening.

Are You a Victim?

We all have a little victim inside of us. We have a little voice that sometimes says, "Poor me." Like anger, a little self-pity can be our higher self, our intuition inspiring us, pushing us to reach for more, to get more out of life. A little self-pity is not an issue as long as it is fleeting.

In contrast, some people make being a victim who they are. Everything they do, everything they think revolves around that identity. Does your attitude resonate the following? "Life is hard. Why can't I get a lucky break? I am sick of being in debt! I am a loser. I have no control over my life. Life is cruel. I don't want to go to work. Everyone else is happier. Why me? I'll never be a success. I'm too fat. No one is nice to me. I never have time to myself. What sort of life is this? I feel sorry for myself. I am so tired. There must be more to life. It's just so hard!"

A victim is someone who blames other people for his or her life and situations instead of being accountable for his or her actions.

So why does a person stay in this role? Why do victims participate in such a limiting habit? They may need to feel blameless. They may need to feel free of responsibility. They may not be able to emotionally cope with pressures associated with responsibility. Anger forms a central part of the victim's identity. Victims take no responsibility and blame everyone and everything else. They feel angry at the world and hold grudges, keep score, and stew over their resentments. Because they hold the belief that "life is out to get them" in their consciousness, this ends up being their reality. In some cases, the only positive attention victims may receive is sympathy. Sympathy from strangers, neighbours, people on public transport, doctors, nurses. They may not have productive, giving, and loving relationships, and they may crave the sympathy, which is a form of attention and a form of energy, so this sympathy can become addictive.

And while many victims pray for change, the change has to start with them. There is nothing wrong with prayers, but they need to be the success, the difference in their lives. The changes need to start in their mind and then filter through to their lives. When victims become accountable for their lives, when they forgive freely, they begin to heal. When they let go of the past, focus on enjoying each present moment, and create a positive future in their mind, their lives will improve.

Many victims are focused on negative, so they keep attracting negative. The victim cloak is a hard one to remove, and therefore, many victims don't change. Because victims blame everyone else—parents, bosses, ex-spouses, children—for their lives, they take no responsibility. They are usually full of resentment and bitterness and do not easily forgive. They do not let go of their past. They over-focus on past hurts and may spend hours and hours focused on the wrongs that have been done to them, and work on ways to "get even." When they understand how life really works, the law of attraction, and that life is not happening to them—*they are creating their life*—they can take back their power and begin to heal. They can have the life of their dreams once they take off the "victim glasses" and change their mindset and take their power back.

Don't Blame Others—It Gives Your Power Away

One of my favourite sayings is, "We are born alone, and we will ultimately leave this earth alone, so we are responsible for our happiness." I feel sad when I meet people who are being controlled or blaming another person for their lives. As part of my relationship counselling checklist, I ask: What are you doing for yourself? What hobbies do you have for *you*?

Being in a relationship doesn't mean we need to give away our life. It means we are sharing our lives with someone we love. If things are not right, we need to stop blaming other people and stop blaming the world. We need to take inventory of our actions to be accountable, to ask what thoughts could have contributed to the issue, or what didn't go the way we planned. What actions did we take or not take? What are we doing? How are we part of the problem? Once we take full responsibility for our lives, then we have the power to change. We are powerless if we think that our lives are a result of other people. To hold our power, we need to know we cannot blame others. We are responsible!

Forgive

We have all heard the words, "There is power in forgiveness." We all know that to forgive others is how to improve our lives. Forgiveness is magical.

Kerrie had a very difficult and hurtful marriage break-up. She then spent years being distant toward men, fearful she may be hurt again. Kerrie's relationship was so abusive that she felt she'd never be able to trust a man again. She was always fearful, assuming any men she met would always have a hidden agenda, that they were all painted with the same brush. In a deep way, Kerrie did not respect men.

Kerrie sought counselling, and when she was ready, she participated in a gestalt "empty chair" technique: She imagined her ex-husband in the chair opposite her, and she closed her eyes and told him she finally forgave him for the way he treated her. She changed chairs and visualized the relationship through his eyes, and she saw what he may have seen. She swapped chairs again and told him, "I forgive you with love, and let you go with love."

She left the session feeling happy but relatively unchanged. Weeks later, Kerrie went to drop her teenage son off at football practise for the first time. She was surrounded by men of all ages. Normally she would be scared, annoyed, judging and dodging any contact … but she just saw a group of men—not bad men … just men. She knew at that moment she was healed. There was great power in the act of her forgiving her ex-husband. She no longer views all men as bad. She once again has respect for all humans, not just the female ones!

To move forward is to forgive with love. We don't have to forget, but we heal when we forgive. Forgive for yourself, not for the other person.

Children

Our interactions with our children make or break them for life. Our children are really given to us on loan; they are our little miracles, and while they may be small, they are simply little adults evolving. Our impact on them will affect their personality, self-concept, self-esteem, and ultimately, their entire life. We are always learning. I hope these simple tips help make this relationship easier and more productive.

What Do Children Need from Their Parents?

1. *Children need daily positive input.* Every interaction with your child hinders or develops their self-esteem. It is vital to ensure your children develop high self-esteem. According to author, Elizabeth Hartley-Brewer, in her excellent book, *Positive Parenting: Raising Children with Self-Esteem*, this high self-esteem will enable your children to be highly motivated, achieve well, and be confident and successful in life. Parents need to give children constant love and affection, reward them, listen to them, get enthusiastic about their activities, and provide a loving, peaceful, and consistent environment.

    You need to show them respect and give them a chance to respect you, by knowing they can rely on Mum and Dad. If you make a promise—keep it. Children need to know that Mum and Dad mean what they say, that their words have weight. Then they can respect you for following through. Children need our affection; they need our hugs and kisses. Our children need to hear, "I love you," from us, and they need to feel that love daily. Children need lots of praise. Children need to know that if we are disciplining them, we are being critical of *their actions*—not them.

    In this relationship you need to give your child, first and foremost, your attention. Spend quality time with them (at least thirty minutes of undivided attention daily). It's not quantity but quality that counts. Children need 100 percent of quality attention when you interact with them. If you cannot talk for a moment, let them know, and then give them the time later. Constantly show them how special they are by giving them your time.

2. *Children need to be given freedom to be themselves.* Children excel when they are allowed to express themselves as individuals, when they are involved in decision making. We need to be empathetic, encouraging their talents and creativity. We need to invest time and money in supporting their interests, and show faith in their abilities and confidence in them overall.

3. *Children need clear communication.* When giving instructions, be clear and positive while mentally preparing your children. Our role as parents is to teach our children about life. We need to ensure we give our children clear directions and warn them of dangers, ensuring we talk in a language that befits the child, so he or she can understand. Then ask the child to repeat the request, if needed, to ensure he or she understood.

   Direct communication is best. Children always feel more secure when they are told beforehand where they are going, what they are doing, and what to expect. Mentally preparing your child for holidays, outings, events, parties, etc., will reduce their anxiety, which equates to a better behaved child.

4. *Children thrive with boundaries and household rules.* Children benefit by having healthy boundaries. Tell your children what you expect from them, and ensure there are consequences that are reinforced. Your child will feel safer, respect you more, and have fewer discipline issues if you set and maintain good boundaries.

   Some parents form the habit of making threats that cannot be carried out. So if you are going to make threats, be prepared to enforce the consequences. For example, if you tell your child that he is not going to receive pocket money if he keeps his room messy, you need to cancel his pocket money that week if he ignores you. Otherwise he will quickly learn that your words mean nothing, and he will continue to have a messy room. Also, having house rules will ensure children are given the opportunity to be responsible and part of the team.

5. *Don't let your children become bored.* I have read that rats would rather push a lever repetitively to feel an electrical current than be bored. Similarly, children would rather irritate you and be told off than be bored. A bored child is often a disruptive child, seeking a parent's attention—even if the attention is negative. Children need a lot of mental stimulation. If you do not ensure they are entertained, you may end up being their entertainment, which will prove to be exhausting after a while.

6. *Work with their fluctuating energy.* Children have a strong need to exercise and can easily seem hyperactive, so it is best to factor these energy changes in when on outings or on holidays. If you are trapped in a car for hours, make a stop at a park so your children can play. Similarly, children become exhausted easily, and we need to be empathetic and factor their energy changes into our routine. An exhausted or hyperactive child can be stressful, so think and plan ahead.

7. *Children are sponges.* Children are products of their environment. Children learn very quickly through modelling, so we need to be careful in relation to their television watching, as even violent cartoons can teach children violence. Children imitate others and learn from observation at a very fast rate. For this reason, we need to think of our children as sponges of information and watch their sources carefully.

We also need to always model appropriate behaviour, as we are a constant source of new information. According to psychologist B. F. Skinner, founder of operant conditioning, children learn through the following reinforcements: positive reinforcement (e.g., a gold star, praise, a reward for good behaviour), and negative reinforcement (e.g., a child keeps his room tidy to avoid a negative consequence of reduced pocket money or having his or her iPod confiscated). In positive reinforcement the child receives something for good behaviour and in negative reinforcement the child has something taken away, in most cases, for poor behaviour. Instead of punishing your child with verbal abuse or put downs, look into ways of teaching your child through daily reinforcements.

8. *How to parent poorly:* Elizabeth Hartley-Brewer created two parenting circles in her book, *Positive Parenting: Raising Children with Self-Esteem.* One circle is entitled *The Positive Circle.* The other is entitled *The Negative Circle,* which lists many of the following unhelpful parenting habits: Poor parenting includes making threats but not carrying them out, so the child simply misbehaves. It also includes instilling fear, rarely praising, criticizing weaknesses, not being affectionate, not investing time with your child, manipulating your child, transferring your feelings of failure to your child, controlling your child through excessive use of power, being quick to punish, yelling at your children, abusing them, blaming them for your moods, making them feel guilty, ignoring them, and showing your children no respect.

The Beauty of Grandparents

I clearly remember my grandma. When I was a teenager, I would catch the train to her house, and when I arrived she would hand me an iced coffee with ice cream, and a sprinkling of nutmeg, and ask me questions about school, boys, and my life. She would intently listen to everything I had to say. When I was in her presence I felt so special. I felt as though there was nothing else Grandma wanted to do but listen to me.

This is the kind of listening we all need to do. To listen well, we all need to stop the internal dialogue, stop what we are thinking about, stop preparing the next question or our next thought. Just listen. Our minds need to be empty, focused only on what we are being told. When we listen and pay attention, we show respect and love. Our relationships are transformed when we give absolute attention to our partners, children, friends, colleagues, and our fellow human beings. To make someone feel special is to listen to him or her and give our fullest attention. If we could all be a little more like our grandmas—with all their time and focus—this world would be a much better place.

We Have a Special Relationship with Nature

Nature plays an important part in our health, our serenity, many of our holidays, and most of our homes. The act of sitting down and enjoying a garden is good for our bodies. In fact, the act of enjoying nature, for example sitting in a forest, in a garden, opposite a large lake, has been shown to actually increase the energy level in our bodies.

Similarly, many experiments suggest we can improve the health of our plants just by giving them attention, talking to them, and sending them love. Some experiments suggest plants respond to various people differently, and even grow differently, depending on the types of music played around them. Plants respond to changes in the environment, and similarly, they respond to us. Numerous tests have been performed where two plants have been given the same amount of water, sun, and nutrients, but one plant has been given lots of loving energy, and the other one lots of negative, angry energy. The plant given the loving energy thrives, yet the one given the negative energy suffers, and in some cases, dies. So there is more to being a "green thumb" than skill ... plants appreciate your love. In return, they give you increased physical energy and loads of joy.

Homework—Are You Listening to Your Relationships?

1. Can you see any of the following unhelpful communication patterns in your family: high conflict, fused, disengaged, coalition, triangulation, or scapegoat?

2. If a positive attitude is vital to your relationship's success, take a moment to examine your attitude. Does your relationship make you happy? What are your expectations? What is your general opinion of your partner? Are your attitudes positive?

3. Considering that you need to "argue well" to be in a happy relationship, do you know all of the steps?

4. Why do children thrive with boundaries yet often misbehave when bored?

5. Why is a healthy self-esteem, in children and adults, so important? How can you help your children have a healthy self-esteem? List five ways.

6. Do you see yourself as a victim? What makes you a victim, and how can you change this?

It takes no special act of providence to fulfil desires; the universal field of existence has been designed to operate for that purpose; if it were not so designed, you couldn't wiggle your toes, blink your eyes, or carry out any mind-body command.—Deepak Chopra

The universe is built to respond to our consciousness, but it will give back to us only the level of quality that we put in.—James Redfield

CHAPTER 7

ARE YOU LISTENING TO LOVE AND PASSION?

The power of love is paramount in your life. For without love—love for self, family, friends, pets, and for what we do—life would be meaningless. The giving of love brings comfort to our souls, fills us with joy, and helps unite humanity. What in this world compares to the feeling of *love*?

When You Love Life, Life Loves You Back!

One of the most amazing things about life, about love, and even about our career is that our mindset, our attitudes, affect everything.

For years I've been telling couples to find another couple as their mentor, a role-model relationship they can look up to, and then to project that couple's positive attitude into their own relationship. When you expect to have the relationship you desire, your relationship is more likely to align itself from there. Having vague or negative expectations will surely set you up for failure. View your partner as Mr./Ms. Romantic! Mr./Ms.

Amazing! Mr./Ms. Everything to me. See your needs being met and they will be. See your work as a place where you go to make the amount of money that you need to support yourself and your family, in the fulfilment of your dreams. Have that expectation, that attitude.

I love what I do. I love life. It is not just a matter of saying it. It is putting it out there as an expectation, and if you don't love your life, *make changes* so that you can love your life, your career, your hobbies, and your relationships.

Our experience on earth is profoundly more enjoyable when we love our life. So surely loving our life is our most important goal?

Surround Yourself with Love

When we love our environment (where we live and work), it becomes a basis for incredible daily joy. If you don't like your home, where you work, or your neighbourhood, make the changes required, both physically and mentally.

I have beautiful friends, Peter and Liz, who live in a small, modest home, and whenever I visit I feel an abundance of love.

They are always redecorating with new cushions, new curtains, different wall colours, and new vases. There is always such a wonderful energy in their home. It's really blissful to be around them. Their home is not big, and they don't have a lot of money, but it's a house full of love.

Look around your home. Is there anything you don't love about it? Does it need your attention? Does it look as though it's lacking love? How do you feel at home? Does your home make you feel happy? You can make changes to this sanctuary, your escape from life. Everything in your home should make you feel good. Different colours affect our energy and how spaces throughout the home feel. Feng shui (pronounced *fung shway*) is also a worthwhile concept to consider when decorating. This Chinese system uses laws of heaven and earth to improve our life and is based on qi (often translated as *chi*), which has been translated as "vital life force" in the human body. So if your home or office feels draining, maybe it is. Look into the wonders of feng shui, balance, the power of colours, and the importance of furniture placement to improve your energy and mood.

Is there enough love displayed in your home? Do you display photos of loved ones? Do you have a space for your trophies? Is your home well organized and a place of peace and joy, or does it feel cluttered? You don't have to be rich to have a house filled with love. If you don't love your neighbourhood, you can move house, or focus your attention on the beautiful people and features in your area.

Loving your workspace is also vital to your success. Could you improve your desk placement or the items on your desk? Is your work area tidy? Does it feel like a loving, peaceful, and productive environment? Do you feel happy at work? If you don't feel happy, make the changes required to make it a place of joy. Love, love, love … surround yourself with love.

Often, love starts from your attitude, so fall in love with your car, house, workspace, family, and friends. The more you love the spaces where you live and work and the people you spend time with, the happier and more successful you will be.

Be an Eternal Optimist—Love and Decode Issues

Our issues are our teachers. They are opportunities for learning and growth. When things go wrong, we can benefit by looking past the issue to try and learn from the message, so we can become more spiritually in tune so our life may improve even more.

We all have issues and have annoying things happen to us. We all make mistakes, make unhelpful choices, and become disappointed. Sometimes life just seems all wrong. So do you feel like your glass is half-full or half-empty? Sometimes it is *not* enough to simply be optimistic. We need to go deeper. We benefit by seeking the "message" and by learning. From losing our keys to losing our jobs, *the universe is always speaking to us.* If we are able to distance ourselves and understand how we (our thoughts and actions) may have contributed to the events, we may eventually be able to see the good side of our challenges, and learn from them, so we can improve our lives.

Part of creating a healthy distance and looking for the part we may have played in the problem stems from acceptance. We accept that an issue exists. The universe is always talking to us, and especially in our setbacks, our issues, and our challenges. So what is the universe saying to you?

Animals Give Unconditional Love

A pet, such as a family dog, can be a constant companion to anyone who needs some love. We humans thrive on attention. We all try to receive attention from our loved ones, yet the family dog simply wants to shower you with attention, morning and night. He is not too busy to notice you; he is not distracted. He wants to show you how much he loves you; whether it be a wagging of the tail or a lick of the hand, your dog is loyal and consistent in his attention giving and love. He loves you and everyone in your family without exception. Having a pet gives you an opportunity to love another "being" on this planet, to love deeply, profoundly, and daily. The act of loving another, whether human or an animal, is to increase love in ourselves. When we increase love within ourselves, we become a magnet for good experiences, good people, and a good life. So having a pet is an opportunity to enrich our life as we increase the love in our life.

Numerous studies have also shown health benefits for the elderly and sick from having a cat or dog. Having a pet encourages mobility, socializing with others, and it is great for self-esteem as the pet loves you unconditionally. Having a pet may reduce isolation and feelings of loneliness. A pet provides companionship and the feeling of being needed, and a chance for us to laugh at ourselves and our pet. Having a pet can reduce stress on a daily basis, promoting better mental and physical health. And, of course, giving your children a pet allows them an opportunity to learn responsibility and to care for an animal, and most importantly, to be part of the cycle of love between humans and animals.

The findings from a ten-year study of more than forty-three hundred Americans suggests that the stress relief pets provide humans is heart-healthy! Accessed March 12, 2013. http://health. usnews.com/usnews/health/healthday/080221/cats-help-shield-owners-from-heart-attack.htm.

Taryn was being tested for breast cancer and was feeling stressed waiting for the results of her mammogram. She sat down, opened a magazine, and to her relief saw a picture of a beautiful horse, almost identical to her beloved horse, Tom, who had passed away years ago. She had loved Tom for eighteen years, since she was fourteen, and that picture in a magazine bought her a sense of calmness … she believed everything would be okay—and it was. The doctor told her she had normal breast tissue. Taryn rushed home and told her family the great news. Taryn felt great comfort in the belief that Tom, her first best friend, the horse all her children rode, was standing strong beside her in spirit on this day, the day she needed his strength, his courage, and his memory!

Love is like a boomerang; it just keeps coming back to you. When you give love, it flows back to you, and the more you give, the more love you feel. You can never run out of love.

Know Your Heart

Every person on this earth has a desire, something he or she wants to achieve, a purpose, a reason for being. Some of these desires are things we conjure up in our minds—to be part of our "wildest dreams" list. Some inspirations are things we want to get to one day, and some are presently being worked on. For many people these desires seem to be suppressed. When I ask my clients, "What do you want to do with your life? What are your desires?" many don't know. We have desires come through to us, sometimes as hunches, inclinations, fantasies, and when we work on these desires, regardless of how long it takes, it fulfils us.

If we have an inclination, and we feel excited, often that is all we need to pursue that passion. Try it out. Move in the direction of that goal, and if it works out—great! If not, work on finding another hobby or interest. I often say to my friends that writing is the chocolate of my life. What is the chocolate of your life? Without chocolate in our life, how can it be sweet?

Discovering and working on our desires excites us, gives us energy, structure, and a purpose for our life. When we follow our passions it exhilarates us; when we ignore our passions, when we put them aside, we may feel oppressed and deeply saddened. Following our passions, therefore, is a key to happiness. Our dreams, visions, and inspirations are our possibilities. When we create our dreams in our mind, almost nothing can stop us, except lack of self-belief, lack of passion, and lack of action.

Spend Thirty Minutes a Day on Your Desires—Keep Your Dreams Alive!

It can change our lives if we spend thirty minutes a day working towards our goals. It can transform your body, it can transform your relationship. Thirty minutes! When you spend thirty minutes a day connecting with your partner, intimacy levels increase, the friendship blossoms, resentment is reduced, and affairs are less likely to happen because you are continually connecting and strengthening the bond. This advice is especially helpful for a couple in relationship crisis. It is great to spend thirty minutes a day giving our children our undivided attention. Of course we spend hours and hours with them, but thirty minutes undivided attention when we just enjoy them is so wonderful for our relationship with our children. We may go to their room if they are young and play games with them in their space. We could listen to their reading, or read to them, and just become part of their world for thirty minutes. What an honour. To have children and not enjoy them is a common tragedy. When we spend thirty minutes a day on our desires, we are more likely to feel as though we are achieving something.

Whether it is studying, working toward what we want, or searching the web for what we need, it is rewarding to know we are on our path and following a direction. It is not just a matter of enjoying our lives; to be fulfilled we need to work on our passions, and listen to our inner voice, our inner needs. If you are unsure what you are passionate about, try thinking outside the circle. Ask yourself, "What would I do if I had six months to live?" This exercise gives us the opportunity to put dreams into perspective. Whether your passion is gardening, exercising, motorbike riding, writing a book, learning to play an instrument, or scrap booking, keeping these passions alive doesn't take a lot of time. So practice the thirty-minute rule in your life and watch how life expands. Spending at least thirty minutes a day dedicated to your passions will take your happiness to the next level!

Visualize

One of the most important factors in achieving our goals is to stand back, brainstorm, even use a whiteboard and then visualize our life's projects and dreams. We need to stop, discuss, and analyze for the best possible end result. What are our goals? Are we working towards our goals? What do we want to achieve? Whether these goals are small or large, visualize the goals as already achieved—and then enjoy the feeling of the end results. The feeling of what that is like. I have been using this "magical" mind-power exercise for many years. Part of this process may be a dream board, where we pin pictures and ideas for our goals. This helps keep us focused on our goals. There is indisputably magic in the power of visualizing. Visualizations work well in many events such as building a house, starting a new career, thinking about a promotion, or when starting a business venture.

An important part of creating a successful relationship is to visualize it first. Whatever we are doing, we need to look at the end result. So if there is anything you want, visualize it, brainstorm it. Spend time thinking about what you want. Get out a diary, write down what you want, and really be in that future moment, enjoying your achievement. Then watch how fast the universe points you in that direction.

We need to co-create tomorrow with the universe. It's like putting in a job application with the universe. It's like saying, "I want this job, I am ready for this new role; please tell me when it becomes available. Thank you."

The Power of Setting Goals

Every single day we evolve and are working to improve our current situation. As we are goal-oriented individuals, we are always focused on what we want next, from the new car to the pay raise to the holiday. We are always working toward some huge goal, but when we really stop and think, life is about all the special moments we create and savour along the journey.

Here are five important elements to consider when working toward achieving our goals:

1. *Passion:* We need to be inspired and excited; the universe responds to thought *plus* enthusiasm.
2. *Faith:* We need to believe our success is possible. Even better if we believe our success is inevitable, as faith is a key ingredient in success.
3. *Visualize:* We need to taste our success. We need to visualize the end result and savour each moment, even before success happens.
4. *Work backward:* We need to decide what we want, and then look at the steps between where we are and where we want to be. By working backward from the goal to where we are today, we can ensure we comprehend (and factor in) all we need to do.
5. *Bite-size pieces:* We need to "chunk it." We need to work toward our goals, in manageable pieces, until we get there. Every huge goal in life really boils down to "what can I achieve today?" or "what can I achieve in the next three hours?".

What type of goals do you have? While we may have career, relationship, and financial goals, we really need to have a more thorough list—life goals. I currently have twelve life goals, and I review these often. I am particularly aware of my number-one goal in life, the most important goal to me, to have daily peace and joy. So when I work toward my relationship, career, family, or social goals, I work at maintaining peace and joy. I make sure my goals do not clash. In practical terms, when I am organizing events in my diary, I work on structuring everything so that my peace and joy are maintained. In the past, I have been wound up over my goals, leaving me feeling inadequate, annoyed, and impatient, as if now became less important than the future. This is where goal setting can work against us. Nowadays I break my goals down into manageable daily goals. I find daily goals so much better than simply focusing on yearly goals. *Now* is the most important time in our life, as life is always in the now.

Be Happy Now!

Are you someone who feels compelled to control? Do you try to control what family members are doing, your own life, time, weight, emotions, career, or goals? Do you get frustrated when your goals do not work out the way you expected? After all, you put it out there—why didn't it happen? It's frustrating when changes occur, when responsibilities just jump out at you and disrupt your carefully planned schedule. This is not a fun, relaxing way to live.

Life can become frustrating when we try to control everything, when we become obsessed by rigid goals. It is far more enjoyable to have broader goals and then release them to the universe. It is helpful to understand that we don't have power over all events and that everything happens for a reason, from small annoyances, like a traffic jam, to larger life-changing events such as an unexpected job loss. There is a deeper meaning to all events; often we cannot see this at the time, and sometimes we will never know why. It helps if we have faith that everything in our life is turning out for our greater good. Being a "control freak" is a frustrating way to live, with little reward. We cannot really control much at all. *The future is not here, so how can we control it?*

When our current goals are achieved, we all seem to create new goals. For this reason, we need to enjoy the journey. Our whole life is the journey. When we achieve our goals, we are always creating another, so the journey is all there is—we never arrive. How is your journey going? We need to be happy *now*, not when we achieve our goals, as we always find more goals to strive toward.

We cannot afford to put our happiness in a future moment (and not in *this* moment) by saying:

I will be happy when I finish my studies.
I will be happy when I leave home.
I will be happy when I secure a job.
I will be happy when I have a partner.
I will be happy when we own our home.
I will be happy when I lose weight.
I will be happy when the weekend is here.

We benefit by being happy *now*. We can cause great unhappiness, dissatisfaction, and dysfunction in our self, and our lives, by not accepting ourselves and our progress as it is *in this moment*. We need to be happy in this moment. Goals are important, but do not let them rule or ruin your life, or make you feel that a future moment is more important than this one. Now is the most important moment you have.

By focusing on what we can achieve this hour, this day, and this week, our life becomes more fulfilling and spirit-led. We can use our intuition and break our goals down into bite-size pieces. Today's goals create tomorrow's success. Be grateful, proud, and happy, and enjoy the journey. Life is a journey and not a destination.

Do Your Best

In my teens, I went to this lovely lady for singing lessons. She would often say to me, "Do your best! The angels can't do better." This is something that has stuck with me. It is so easy to strive for perfection, to almost go crazy over the details, and to obsess. It's such a natural thing to sit at a desk hour after hour, ignore thirst, ignore hunger, to try to finish our work, aiming for perfection. I like to think of my singing teacher at these times. *All we can do is our best.* Most people do the best they can, at the time, and their best is good enough. Your best is all you can do. If you are aiming for what is not possible, you will end up frustrated, miserable, angry, and disappointed with yourself.

Perfectionism is trying to achieve the impossible—for what in this world is perfect? In my life, my marriage, my work, I do my best and I'm happy with that. I know my relationships are not perfect, but they are fulfilling and amazing. Nor is my life perfect, but it is an exciting adventure. I give the best I can on that day, or in that moment, which is all I can ever do. All we can do is aim for something achievable and do our best.

Planet Thinking

Twice a month I do some "planet thinking." Now, planet thinking is not your everyday thoughts. Planet thinking is where you pretend you are sitting on another planet, and looking all the way down to earth, and then you look at yourself, your life, your goals, and everything you have been doing lately and analyze it all. But you do not do it from your perspective. No. You do it from an "outsider's" perspective, as if you were analyzing someone else's life. You need to be objective. It is amazing! I have made profound discoveries during planet thinking. I have discovered (and improved) so much about myself, my habits, and my life and I love it! The interesting thing about planet thinking is that it is a very different state of mind that creates such intense clarity of thought; details become crystal clear, whereas they may not have been before. You can planet think in the bath, on a deck chair, on your couch—anywhere. Being aware of your habits is part of being able to change them. Become more aware of your habits, and move forward with a little planet thinking!

Tips for planet thinking:

1. Sit down with a warm or cold drink.
2. Ensure you will not be interrupted.
3. Ensure you have plenty of time, as you do not want to feel rushed.
4. Think about your goals and your life (relationships, family, fitness, work, etc.) from an outsider's perspective.
5. Ask yourself these four questions about your life using an outsider's perspective:
    a. What is going well in this person's life?
    b. What is *not* going well in this person's life?
    c. What improvements can be made, in relation to attainment of this person's goals?
    d. What new strategies or time-management systems can be implemented?

Master Yourself—Master This World

Are you happy with how you feel each day? Are you happy with the way you look? Do you bounce out of bed with vitality each day? Do you have energy, enthusiasm, and well-being powering you, making you feel as though you can achieve anything?

If you don't feel this way, then analyze your activities and your life. Do you usually have self-discipline, as do all successful businessmen and businesswomen? It starts with their daily ritual, which normally incorporates a balance of work, exercise, healthy eating, recreation, and relationships. We can get out of bed at 6:30 a.m. and exercise, we can plan a healthy eating menu, and we can treat our bodies like temples. Self-discipline is so important. We need to think about what we want, how we can achieve it, and then make our daily activities reflect these goals.

We can't just let life happen to us. Self-discipline is really time management, having a routine, planning ahead, thinking of the goal—making our day reflect the person who we are, making daily rituals that keep our bodies and our minds in excellent working states. If we are studying or completing projects, self-discipline is putting the time in, focusing on what we need to achieve, and structuring our life so that we are working toward our goals every day. Without self-discipline we drift and our goals are not achieved.

Self-discipline can be as simple as completing our hardest tasks first, going to bed early, getting up that little bit earlier, and structuring our week to achieve the utmost!

Homework—Are You Listening to Love and Passion?

1. List everything you love in your personal and professional lives. Make any necessary changes to your home and workplace so you can enjoy your life more.
2. List all the people you aspire to be like. What characteristics do you admire in them?
3. Your problems talk to you; they teach you about yourself and life.
   Draw up four columns:
   a. Column 1: Problems: List all your recent problems.
   b. Column 2: Response: List all contributing actions/thoughts.
   c. Column 3: Lessons: Can you see any underlying messages or lessons?
   d. Column 4: Help: Identify the strategies that helped you make positive changes.
4. Know your heart. If you believed you could not fail, what would you attempt to do, personally and professionally? Daydream … expand your mind and then write the list.
5. Make a list of your goals:
   a. What are your twelve life goals?
   b. What do you want to achieve in the next twelve months?

    c. What do you want to achieve in the next five years?

    d. If you were told you had six months to live, what would you want to do before you died?

6. Are you spending at least thirty minutes a day on your goals?

Time is seen as the endless succession of moments, some "good," some "bad." Yet if you look more closely ... you find that there are not many moments at all. You discover that there is only ever this moment. Life is always now.—Eckhart Tolle

Both poverty and riches are the offspring of thought.—Napoleon Hill

CHAPTER 8

ARE YOU LISTENING TO TIME AND MONEY?

There is Only Ever One Moment—Now!

Life is in the details. My life was changed some years ago when I first read the words of Eckhart Tolle. His books *Stillness Speaks: The Power of Now* and *A New Earth* taught me about living in the moment, of not endlessly worrying or thinking about the future, and to stop dwelling on or reliving the past. I learned to live every moment to the fullest. This completely transformed the way I live: I became present. I often recommend *The Power of Now* to my clients. Mindfulness is a special technique that brings awareness into our present moment.

When we live in the present, we are changed. It is powerful—we give to everything we do. We take in our surroundings and focus on what we are doing. We are not missing out on anything. Our relationships are transformed because we are listening, focusing, giving attention, loving. Our careers blossom, as we are not getting lost in the details—we are immersed in them and are passionate. Our capacity for happiness improves as our life becomes a passionate encounter, full of intensity, from one moment to the next. When we stop the endless mind chatter and become present, miracles happen. I cannot state enough the power of focusing on the current moment ... on this moment, and on each following moment. The quality of our life is directly related to the quality of the attention we give to each moment. Try it for yourself and see.

Sacred Morning Minutes

The moment you wake every morning, spend a few minutes planning your day. How can you spend your time today to achieve the best possible outcome? While you are half-asleep, your subconscious mind is "half-open," and in this state you can plan the best possible day. Since I have been doing this, my productivity has soared. I ponder what needs to be achieved over the next twelve hours, and I turn my whole living, my goal setting, into just this day.

What can you achieve this day? How will you plan this day, hour by hour, to achieve the most? I call this my sacred time, as I believe that we are more easily influenced by our spiritual guides, angels, and our intuition when we have just woken. For some time, I have been turning some decisions or issues over to my guides and have woken up on a couple of occasions with profound answers and suggestions from seemingly out of nowhere. Sometimes we may hear a sentence, sometimes we just get a certain "feeling" that helps us make a decision or solve a puzzle in our lives. So whether it's planning our day or seeking spiritual guidance, these first moments in the morning are so special.

Pockets of Time—How to Achieve More in Less Time
© Phoebe Hutchison 2013

We benefit by structuring our lives and our time if we want the best results in work and play. Structure includes time for exercise, for work, to socialize, and to reflect. Often friends ask me, "How do you do it? How do you run a company, work as a counsellor, promote one book while writing a second, record a CD, run a household, and be a mum?" I use a trick I call "pockets of time." I never waste time, I am never bored, and I am only ever in one of two zones: work or socializing/relaxing. My friends and family know not to call me for a long chat during work hours, and I rarely work after 5:00 p.m. During my nights I am socializing and relaxing.

My whole life is just pockets of time. I divide up the day and the week, and whatever I am doing I focus only on that task. I give 100 percent to everything I do; one thing at a time, as this is the best way to achieve quality results. When I work, I rarely listen to the radio, I only do my job. When I am sitting at my desk, I am working. When I am with counselling clients, I am one 100 percent focused on them. When I am doing the weekly housework, I have my tracksuit on, the music is loud, and my goal is to work fast, while enjoying the music. When I knock off work, I focus entirely on my family, relaxing/socializing, and when I relax on a Friday night, I have a glass of champagne, order take-away food, and watch a video with the family or enjoy a BBQ with friends and family. I do not cook. Similarly, Saturday nights are all about relaxing. Whether cleaning the house, exercising, working on a book, or shopping, I set the time aside and give everything to that pocket of time.

If you run a business from home, feel easily distracted at your workplace, or if your productivity is low and you are not sure where your time is going, this log on/log off technique should help. As soon as you begin working at your job, open a text box or spreadsheet on your computer or phone, or grab a notepad, and log your start time. If you stop to chat, work on personal matters, check your Facebook, or stop for any break, note a log off time. When you resume your work, enter a new start time. Then, add up all your hours at the end of the day and week. This exercise should keep you focused on your work and make you aware of how many hours you actually worked per week. (You could add a description of the different areas you worked on, to establish time spent on each task.) Nowadays, I use this same log on/log off technique while working on my book. I get up and walk around and have a break every hour or so to remain mentally fresh. This technique should help you stay in work mode, increase your productivity, and bring awareness to time spent on different tasks.

Managing our time is important just hour by hour, a day at a time. We need to be present and not let our whole life, our past, our future take over this day—our day. We can "send out" to the universe just what we want to achieve, and if the gentle winds of the universe wish to quietly change our plans, that's fine. If we don't create our day, everyone else's plans can quickly take up our time and interrupt our aims. We all have the same twenty-four hours to achieve; by planning this—our day—we achieve so much more.

All great achievers know that by mastering time, we master our world. When we plan our minutes, hours, and days, we plan our life.

Enjoy the Moments in Between

Life is busy and time is such a funny thing. When you are in a rush and the pace of life feels flat out, you can still take the opportunity to savour the moments in between. Really focus on that tiny amount of peace—even if it is only twenty seconds. These moments are there to be savoured. You may be rushing to complete tasks, or waiting on the phone for someone, just listening to the music. You may be in the car on the way to work. Friends may be coming over, and you are prepared, ready, and waiting and have a few moments to settle your molecules. Just relax and take a deep breath before changing gears and becoming a host. These special moments are always combined with the rush yet can still be enjoyed.

You may have just hurried into the supermarket, knowing your partner is waiting in the car, and notice the only open checkout has four people queuing in front of you. While you could stress, you choose not to. You can simply take a breath, push your fringe back, adjust the heavy basket of groceries, plant your feet firmly, and enjoy the two minutes of utter peace. Focus on people-watching or just gaze into space and think of nothing, or mentally make a checklist of jobs you need to do that day, or on the weekend. This is your two minutes of peace, and you do not have to waste this moment, between the moments, getting angry, worrying about the time, or stressing out like the person behind you (who is dancing from foot to foot, red-faced, and muttering about the slow checkout operator!). No, you are not that red-faced person—you are savouring this moment, like you savour them all! Enjoying these moments will give you a sense of peace and a boost of energy and is great for your mind, body, and soul.

You Have the Ability to Slow Time Down

If you begin to feel like life is getting faster, if you have too many appointments and/or commitments, then take action. *Slow down.* Take some breaths, walk slower, talk slower, and begin to feel calmer. This change in pace should help anchor you in the now, so you can feel more grounded. Even if life starts to feel frantic, by slowing our physical body down, life can slow down too.

Regardless of what is happening around us, if we feel grounded we achieve more. Being grounded is our key to peace and to achievement. So next time you are having a stressful time, look for a quiet place to sit and just relax. Have a glass of water, a piece of fruit, or a small snack, and switch off the world. When you are "on" again in the world, you can then perform at your best. After a twenty-minute break of complete solitude, away from the busy world, you can return and achieve the tasks at hand. Relax, slow down, and find the clarity you seek.

Satori—What a Word!

Are you overly focused on the future or past moments and missing out on the moments right in front of you, the moments in the now?

My mother and I went on a holiday some years ago. Well, anyone who knows me knows I can talk! But if you think *I* can talk, you have to meet my mother. When the two of us holiday every year, we just talk, talk, talk! We talk so much, it can be easy to "miss" the sights because we are so deep in conversation. So we would use the word *satori*, which roughly means "sudden spiritual awakening." Mum and I used this word to shut each other up at times, so we did not miss the scenery. We would be travelling around, driving past beautiful historical buildings, but our minds were back at home. We would be engaged in conversations about the family, what had been happening with friends—everything except this amazing holiday. While we were sitting looking at the beautiful scenery, we may as well have been at Mum's sitting on her floral couches, having a cup of tea.

So every time we drifted off into conversations about "home," one of us would say "satori!," instantly snapping us back into the wonderful reality we were in.

When you are travelling, do you need to remind yourself to stop the endless mind chatter, to be able to enjoy the sights and scenery? Be present so that you don't miss life's experiences.

Your Best Time

Studies have been done on the productivity of humans, and it has been shown that we all have a "best time," a period each day where we are the most focused and enthusiastic and where our brains function at their best. We will achieve more in our lives if we can work within our optimum periods for peak concentration. When I was writing my first book, my best time seemed to be between 7:30 and 9:30 p.m. I felt creative, energetic, and fresh. Nowadays I feel my best time for concentrating seems to be between 9:00 a.m. and 1:00 p.m. I can concentrate best during this time, so I usually perform my most challenging physical and mental tasks during this time. I prefer to relax at night, and by 5:00 p.m. I am not as mentally sharp. Make the most of your best time each day and watch your productivity soar!

The Mystery of Time

Are we going back and forth in time and not realizing it? Have we already lived as our future self? Are we feeling familiarity because we have lived not just in the past, but in the future? Are our future memories in the part of the mind that we cannot access, the percentage that we humans are not using?

Have you ever met someone and thought he or she seemed incredibly familiar? Even though you question each other, trying to find the connection, neither of you can find a reason. You did not go to school together and came from different areas, yet this person seems so familiar. When this happens to me, I often wonder if this person will be in my future, and in most cases, I am right. I view time a little differently than most people do. What if time is *not* the straight line we assume it is? Are we present in every millisecond of our consciousness, or do we flicker in and out? Well, according to some schools of thought, our cells flicker in and out and can be in more than one place at a time. If our cells do this, are we moving? If so, where do we go? Are we visiting the future? And who truly knows what happens when we sleep, where our mind travels to? (Some of our dreams seem very real.)

What about the complexities of past-life associations, if you believe in reincarnation? What about parallel lives and times? One of the greatest minds of our time, Albert Einstein, is believed to have suggested that time is "an illusion". He is quoted as saying the only reason for time is so everything doesn't happen at once. Some theorists believe in timelessness, that all things in the past, present, and future could exist simultaneously. I know these ideas may seem bizarre. Yet how do we explain the feeling that we know someone we have never met? Something about the person's soul, look, or mannerism seems all too familiar.

When we are attracted to certain people and places, and when people and places seem familiar, could there be deeper meanings—deeper than science can currently explain?

Examine Your Relationship with Money

There is a relationship that people don't talk about so much, and this is their relationship with money. How is your relationship with money? Do you treat money like a person who is very close to you, who can help to make dreams come true? Or do you think of money the same way many people do? Is money not treating you well at present? Is money stressful? We all have times when money does not treat us too well—this is our learning process, the school of life teaching us.

Our relationship with money is so significant. The attitude, the energy, is so vital. The law of attraction shows us that we attract the same as the energy we send out. If you always believe that life is a struggle, bills are stressful, there is never enough money, that you will never be rich—then these things are going to be your reality. Many people feel guilty, ashamed, and fearful about money. Some hide behind constant new purchases, as they try to keep up with the latest trend or try to impress other people, yet they feel sick to the stomach when the bills come in. Then there are those people whose credit card debt simply keeps climbing … until they consolidate it with the mortgage and start again. All these attitudes and experiences are negative! I want you to feel powerful, brave, and have fun with money. Money gives you freedom, choices, and can add great excitement to your life, but not if your relationship with money is maladaptive.

So how do you change this relationship? You need to do a 180-degrees turn if it's not working. You need to stop all negative thoughts about money and start loving money. Start treating money with respect, start saving, appreciating the cents, and watching the dollars grow. Are you making purchases you cannot afford and then stressing about paying back the credit card? You need to have honesty in this relationship. Are you lying to yourself, your partner, and everyone? Do you earn enough to cover the bills and your monthly hobbies or entertainment? Are you living beyond your means? These scenarios are so common. Is your relationship with money just like a hamster on the treadmill? Are you moving forward or just using a lot of energy?

Like any relationship, you need to get to know and start listening to money. What is it saying to you? Make a budget. Work out what you spend versus what you earn. Focus on debt reduction, but also factor in some money for you. Set this money aside to enjoy guilt free. Once you have *repaid* your debt (mortgage aside), even if it takes years, then start saving. Save so that you can feel rich, as it's *all* about feelings! Once you have some money set aside, in case of emergency, you *never* have to feel powerless again. I want you to feel powerful, rich, and have fun with money! You can feel rich just by having a small amount of savings in the bank. Once the money you earn is yours to keep (i.e., you have no consumer debt), then you will experience the joys of money.

The problem with most people is that they have credit-card debt, and they make purchases using their credit card (money they don't have), and then they feel guilty. Money has negative energy around it for these people. You earned your money so you can spend it, but you need to be accountable and alleviate debt first, and then you will be free! Seek help from a financial expert and do what you need to do in order to spend *your* money, not the bank's money. If you cannot repay the credit card at the end of the month, then you cannot use it for purchases!

The best advice I ever received about money was from a multimillionaire businessman. He said, "Pay all your bills once a month, so that you do not get behind with your payments." Too many businesses and individuals are paying bills today that were due two months ago. They never feel as though they catch up, adding to their sense of powerlessness and frustration ... just more negative emotions. Need more motivation? Grab your credit-card statements, if you have any, and add up the interest over twelve months. Do you enjoy giving this to the bank? Wouldn't you rather keep this to spend on yourself? And if you can't trust yourself, don't carry credit cards with you—leave them at home. Make the changes, and take *your* power and *your* money back! Get off the "debt treadmill" and enjoy spending again.

A great financial strategy usually results in a healthy bank balance. But ultimately, your finances are never about the dollar you spend but the health of your relationship with money. A healthy, positive, and respectful relationship usually equals a healthy and positive bank balance.

Put Your Relationship with Money to the Test

Our relationship with our finances is just like a relationship with a person. Isn't it time you analyzed this relationship and found the areas where you can make improvements? Do you have a love/hate relationship with money? Does just thinking about money make you feel sick to your stomach? To have increased cash flow you need to examine, and possibly change, your thoughts on money. More money obviously means more choices in life. It is healthy to love and enjoy money. Yet so many people look at the figures and not the corresponding thoughts, beliefs, and feelings around their money situation. I believe money is either physical (stressful) or spiritual (wonderful).

See if you can relate to the two completely different mindsets. One normally accompanies those in debt and struggling financially. The other often accompanies those with great cash flow. In order to increase our spare cash, we need to reduce our debts. However, to increase your income, you also need to have a better relationship with money. Making money starts with your attitude, so if you want more money, you will need to change your attitude. How does your relationship with money look? Which list can you relate to most?

Money Is Stressful	Money Is Wonderful
Making money is hard.	Making money starts with my attitude.
I often feel guilt and shame about money.	I deserve a lot of money.
Debt is a part of life.	I have no consumer debt.
I buy on credit.	I use my money or repay credit monthly.
I have no savings.	I enjoy saving.

There is never enough money.	I am generous as money is plentiful.
I stress about money all the time.	I believe my financial needs will be met.
I envy people who are rich.	I am inspired to learn from others.
I often feel fearful and worried about money.	I feel gratitude for my financial freedom.
I spend impulsively and then I feel bad.	I have a budget—"Do I want or need it?"
I feel self-pity. Why do I have to struggle?	I keep a positive attitude towards money.
I lie to myself and my partner about my expenses.	I never lie about expenses.
I put bills on the fridge as a reminder of debt.	I don't let bills have power over me.
I pay bills almost daily.	I pay my bills once a month.
Being rich is selfish.	I *love* and *adore* money.

Do Not Fear Poverty

Fear is a strong and powerful emotion, and a lot of fearful thoughts will propel you toward the direction of that dominant thought. So to fear something frequently is to point in that direction. We have thousands of thoughts; they come into our minds and then they leave. Sometimes these thoughts are fearful. *What if I lose my job or our money? What if we can't pay the mortgage? What if our business fails?* Fear, like guilt, can also be very harmful in excess amounts.

I treat money with respect and make careful financial choices based on logic, experience, and my intuition, which I trust. Sometimes life is a roller coaster; situations change, and these are lessons we can learn from; some of these lessons are of financial loss. I have faith that our universe will provide for me (and you) always. To overcome fear, I sometimes use an affirmation such as "I am powerful!" or "I trust my intuition and I trust life." I repeat these so I can live the brave life.

Focus on Wealth

My husband and I seemed to be doing well, and then we had an unexpected expense, and then after that came a second unexpected expense, and then we seemed to have more expenses than usual in other areas too. I began to complain to the universe, which I don't normally do as it changes the energy surrounding money. Our relationship with money needs to be positive, even a kind and loving relationship. Generally my relationship with money is without stress. But unfortunately, that month of extra bills rattled me. I began whining to my friends about our expensive month, and then suddenly expenses started coming in from all directions. The car broke down, and a major repair became instantly necessary. We also had a home heating repair, a large expense and just as necessary. Then tradesmen, who had completed some work on our home, also forwarded their account. Lastly, the power company sent us a remarkably huge bill.

It seemed to me that the more I complained, the more bills arrived. I had to stand back and look at this problem, to ask myself what was going on. The final straw came when the washing machine broke down. At last I realized my relationship with money had become negative. I was whining to my friends about the expenses, whining about the accounts, and because I had changed the energy around our money, I was drawing negative energy toward the money, and our expenses increased rapidly.

When I looked to the positives of the situation, I could see that we had the funds to meet these expenses. I am also grateful that this type of month is a rarity. I changed my attitude back to gratitude, stopped complaining, and our expenses returned to normal. I accepted my part in that expensive month, and I have realigned my thoughts so I am once again positive and affirming wonderful cash flow with minimal expenses.

Have Positive Expectations

Use visualization techniques (burn the figures into your mind) for a wage increase or for receiving the price you want for the sale of a car or house. Always set your mind on a higher figure that is still realistic, and patiently, positively, expect that figure to eventuate. Put the figure firmly in your mind; see it clearly and expect it. I have used this technique for more than a decade to increase my business and receive the sale prices we want for our houses, cars, or anything we may sell. Without creating a figure, without letting the universe know what you expect, you are leaving your income to chance.

Belinda lives a modest life, holds a part-time job, and works hard to pay the weekly bills. One day she heard about an upcoming ten million dollar Powerball lottery, so she bought a ticket. She chatted with her co-worker about her ticket, smiled, looked to the sky, waved her hands, and said, "I would be happy with just $100,000, thanks!" To her surprise, Belinda was a Powerball winner. Guess how much she won? One hundred and five thousand dollars. Belinda paid her mortgage off, gave some money to her children, bought her first brand new car, and said thank you to the universe. This win was a testament to Belinda that "something out there is listening to us." I also believe it confirms the power of being specific in our financial goal setting.

We Don't Need to be Millionaires to Enjoy Life

It was a beautiful Saturday, and I was taking my dog for a walk. I was aware of how blue the sky was, how refreshing the gentle breeze felt on my skin, and how the temperature of the air was just right. You know those magnificent spring days? As I walked down the path near my home, I looked to the big eucalyptus trees on both sides, swaying in the breeze, and I felt such intense peace. It was in that moment that I thought, *I don't think someone with millions in the bank could enjoy this moment more than I.* Having millions could not improve this moment.

Everyone, whether they are struggling to make ends meet, in mountains of debt or not, can enjoy the sun on their face, the wind on their cheeks, and most importantly, the love from their family and friends. These pleasures, such as a walk to the park with the kids, a stroll on the beach, or a drive on a sunny day are priceless and available for all to enjoy.

Homework—Are You Listening to Time and Money?

1. You are most powerful in this moment: If you focused on *only* this moment from now on, how could you possibly experience any stress? Is there really any stress in the current moment, if you break it down? Or is your stress related to past moments or fear of future moments?
2. Achieving more with less: Please use the following strategies to increase your efficiency.
   a. Sacred Morning Minutes—plan your day to ensure maximum productivity and balance.
   b. Pockets of Time—divide your day into only work, exercise, rest, or socializing.
   c. Best Time—perform the most difficult tasks when you are at your "peak time."

3. Making time for your goals: Make a list of all you wish to achieve personally and professionally. This may include a health and fitness goal, study, renovating, completing projects, hobbies, or finalizing work tasks. Work out what time will be required per week, then per day, to achieve these goals. Incorporate these goals into your weekly diary and then your Sacred Morning Minutes. You may wish to use some of your peak time for optimum results. With self-discipline, motivation, and planning, you can achieve the best results, in the most practical time frame.

4. Financial Goals: What are your financial goals? Do you want to simply be debt free and own your home? Or do you aspire to own many properties or a successful business? Do you want high cash flow, so you can spend a lot? Or do you simply want enough money to pay the bills with a little left over? Whatever your goals are, make a list and let the universe know.

5. Your thoughts, attitudes, and emotions have a large bearing on your finances. Let's explore these:

    a. When you think about your finances, does this cause stress or satisfaction?

    b. Do you think that being rich will make you happier? If so, list why. If not, list why.

    c. Do you feel like you deserve to be rich? Would you feel guilty if you won a large lottery? Be honest with yourself. How do you feel about people who are rich? Do you envy or admire them?

6. Expand your mind: If your wage was five times higher, how would you spend this extra money? What would you buy? How would you invest the extra funds? Which activities would you do that you are not doing now? Let the universe know where your extra funds will go before your receive them. Plan, expand your mind, enjoy creating wealth with your mind first, and then you will have a greater chance of having wealth in reality.

Learn from yesterday, live for today, hope for tomorrow. The important thing is to not stop questioning.—Albert Einstein

Our life is shaped by our mind; we become what we think. Suffering follows an evil thought as the wheels of a cart follow the oxen that draws it.—Gautama Buddha

CHAPTER 9

ARE YOU LISTENING TO THE RULES?

Life is full of unwritten laws that apply to us all. When we break the rules, life may give us a warning or lesson. If we don't heed the warnings or learn from these lessons, we may become stuck and confused. If we follow the rules and learn from life's lessons, our awareness about our self and our life increases, as does our personal power and capacity for happiness.

Love the Rules and Learn the Lessons

Life is not as mysterious as we may think. As we navigate our way through life we stumble, we fall, and we must learn and grow. Life teaches us, albeit sometimes the hard way, to pick ourselves up and learn from the many lessons we experience. Have you come from the "school of hard knocks"? Do you feel like you have lived through so many changes that you have had more than one life? Have you learned from your lessons? Life teaches us how things can go wrong and cause great anguish and pain. We grow from our lessons in love, money, emotional trials, and addiction.

We can create a new world for ourselves, full of gratefulness, positive visualizations, forward thinking, fulfilling relationships, acceptance, self-love, abundance, and magic. *Life is speaking to you!* Are you ready to listen?

The Universe Will Keep Sending the Same Lessons

The universe will give you the same lesson until *you get it*! If the lesson is very important the universe will send it to you over and over and over again, until you learn from it.

Life is a school and we learn the lessons. The lessons may be about relationships, understanding and managing our emotions, hardship or loss, sickness or pain, our careers, parenting, independence, confidence, detachment, addiction, self-control, and more. Sometimes it takes us a long time to learn the lesson that life is trying to teach us. One lesson may be small, like being late for work because we didn't put petrol in the car the night before. Other lessons may be large, such as a relationship ending, job loss, or financial stress. If we seem to have a lot of stress in one area, if one area in our life needs help, then just like school, we need to "hit the books." We need to seek help, study, network, anything we can do to find the solutions to our issues. We need to honestly evaluate our life, see where we need help, and give this area the attention it needs. If we need help with our finances, we can see a financial planner or counsellor. If we feel like we can't manage our relationship, we can buy a book on relationships or see a counsellor to gain new perspectives and strategies. The lessons usually don't stop until we make a change.

Change is a three-step process:

1. Honestly evaluate the situation.
2. Seek expert advice.
3. Change your attitude and actions.

Is life telling you something? Do you keep coming up against the same issues all the time? If you do, go back to school—the school of life—and learn how to fix the issues once and for all!

You Create Your Own Experiences

You are at the helm of your ship of life. Your role is to steer your ship safely through the storms and sunny days of life. You are in control of this ship. One of the reasons people become unhappy is because they do not take responsibility for themselves. They say, "He won't let me go out. He won't let me spend money. I hate my job. I hate my body. I never have enough money. I hate where I live."

Instead of acknowledging the power they have being the captain of their ship, they blame the water (all their issues). They allow other people to direct their ship of life—to take over (like pirates). They allow other people to steer their ship and rob them of time and energy. They are impacted by the storms of life, they are misguided in a harmful direction, and they do not stop, reassess their maps, and move in the direction they want to go.

Be the captain of your ship of life. Even if you have a spouse, you have a responsibility to yourself (and your spouse) to be the captain of your ship. You are sailing the same course, the same direction, but it is your journey. Your ship of life!

One of our biggest misconceptions is that life just happens to us! It doesn't. Our life is a result of our choices, the choices we make every minute, every day, every week, every month, and every year. If we don't like this life at present, we can create a better future based on better choices.

Your Perception is Powerful

We become angry and frustrated and blame our fluctuating emotions, yet often the *perception of our situation* is to blame. If we change our *perception* of reality, then our emotional reactions will change. In quantum physics it has been shown that atoms change the way they react simply by being observed. Similarly our life quickly changes when we apply attention to viewing our situations differently. (This is similar to affirmations; however, affirmations are more of a long-term solution and can take longer to work.) A simple change in perception can transform our attitude, energy, thoughts, and emotions *in a moment!*

Following are examples of how we can improve our life by simply changing our perception:

Old Perception: My marriage is a real challenge. It is such hard work.

New Perception: I enjoy working on my marriage. I know we have our ups and downs, but it is always improving, and I feel so grateful to have a wonderful partner.

Old Perception: My clients are out to rip my company off. I get so angry when I feel used by them.

New Perception: Most of my clients are great and many become good friends. I feel grateful for their business as without them there is no business.

Old Perception: My life is boring. Nothing seems to interest me anymore.

New Perception: Every day I make myself a priority by thinking about exciting possibilities for my life. I also focus on (and appreciate) my talents, opportunities, and relationships, and they improve.

Have Some "Me" Time Daily

When do you allow yourself to just sit? When do you take a few hours off, and watch your favourite TV show? When do you walk outside, lie down in the sun, read a magazine, and sip tea? What happens at the end of a busy workday? Do you take the children to their activities, do washing and/or shopping, cook, clean, and let the rush continue? Push, push, push—we are always pushing ourselves. The human race works with computers more and more, and I feel like we are treating ourselves like computers more and more—over-scheduling ourselves until we do not get enough breaks.

So many working women have told me over the years how they put away the washing or do ironing at night and clean the house and do weekly shopping on weekends. Not for me—I need sacred time every day, and I like to rest and enjoy life on weekends. Most Sunday to Thursday nights, I insist on a delicious thing called "me" time. After 9:00 p.m. until the time I go to sleep, I do whatever I like. I may read a magazine, watch television or snuggle in bed with my hubby, or watch a movie. *I love my "me" time.* Are you having daily "me" time? It will improve your relationship with yourself and others, and benefit your health, as well as increase your peace and happiness.

Real versus Not Real—Keep It Tangible!

It is not enough to simply have goals, plans, and expectations for ourselves; we need to monitor our progress. We need to be honest with ourselves. All aspects of our life, whether it is our finances, our dreams, or our family relationships need to be measured and realistically viewed. We need to keep it real and be aware of the bottom line.

If we have been on a diet to lose weight for six months, and we have not lost weight, then the diet is not working. We need to change what we are doing. Everything in our life is either working or not working. Is there any area in your life that is currently not working that needs to change? Are your daily habits creating a fit body for you? Are your work habits moving you toward your goals? Are you in the relationship of your dreams? If not, can you think of a way to improve the situation and create a better strategy? Are your actions destroying or building your relationship? How are your relationships with your children? Do you need to read parenting books or attend parenting classes? Do you have financial plans for the future? Are you spending more than you earn? Do you have a household budget?

Grab a diary and start making a list. In behaviour therapy, counsellors work with clients who wish to changes habits. We begin by asking the client to create a baseline, which is a list of their current behaviours. For example, if a client wants to lose weight, a client would list his or her eating and drinking habits for a week. We may ask the client to include the emotional reasons for eating, times he or she eats, types of food, etc. Then using this list, we can honestly see where the issues exist. From this point, from the honest evaluation of actions, we can move forward and work on change. A baseline gives a client the opportunity to see his or her habits written down so he or she can improve them. After the baseline, the client defines a goal that is important, measurable, positive, and attainable. The baseline and detailed goals are a very powerful catalyst for change. The goal stems from an honest, real account of the now.

In order to make positive changes in our life, we must first be honest with ourselves. What we are doing is either working or it's not.

Your Past Is Talking to You

Do you want to know how you can predict the future? It's easy. Just look at your past. Have you always wondered why we study history in school? Now you know. When you stand back and analyze your life; when you look at everything you have achieved; you can get a glimpse into your future! Think this is crazy? Let me explain. Nothing we do is a waste of time. Everything we have done in our life has prepared us for this moment! Have you ever felt that you have just wasted a huge chunk of your life, in a relationship or in a career? Well, nothing is ever a waste, and when we change our thinking, when we compare all we have achieved to all we want to achieve, we can often see patterns.

Why don't you do your own "personal history exercise"? Create four columns, across the page with these headings: Employment, Skills Acquired (or Learning), Like, and Dislikes. Do this for all the various work roles (and voluntary/unpaid positions) you have ever had. Next to each relevant entry write down the skills you acquired, and your likes and dislikes for each of these roles. Now write your goals for your ideal career at the bottom of the page. Can you recognize any patterns? Are there areas where past work roles, which may have seemed insignificant, were actually training you for future employment positions? Our history is important, yet often we forget to acknowledge what we have done.

We minimize the importance of our various roles. Our past work roles have taught us in many ways. They help us better understand our strengths and weaknesses in the workplace, what we want to avoid or seek, and where we excel and shine. When we participate in our own history lesson, we often see glimpses of our future. It's a little magical. You may also wish to do a history lesson for other areas in your life, like your past relationships, houses, hobbies, even your friendships!

An Organized Home Is an Organized Mind

Is your house messy? Is your garage out of control? Is there clutter everywhere? When we have a messy house and feel our environment is out of control, we may feel angry, stressed, or frustrated. These negative thoughts make our minds feel messy, which in turn creates more mess! So, mess creates a never-ending cycle! How do you clean up? Be well organized; have a place for everything; and ensure everything is in its place. I also find it helpful to spend time looking at the mess, mentally going through where I will place it and visualizing walking through all the steps, before tackling the task at hand.

One friend of mine says that after a big cleanup, she feels ready for a new and exciting opportunity. For her, cleaning up and creating more space in her home is synonymous to spiritually preparing for changes in life. When we go through our belongings and give possessions away, we feel lighter and rewarded by simply giving. When we give to others, when we are generous, we feel good. In some way, when we give to others, we receive so much more. If we are not using an item, if it is just gathering dust, we can give it away. Some possessions may hold us back on a deep level, and may serve as unhappy reminders. There is something cathartic about giving things away, throwing items out, and making space in our homes, offices, and lives. A tidy and organized house can lead to a tidy and organized mind, which leads to a tidy and organized life.

Forward Plan—Plan Future Moments

While we need to live in the moment, as this moment is all there is, we benefit by preparing for our future moments. When we save, pay extra off the mortgage, or invest for retirement, we are using forward planning, but this book is not focused on only creating wealth but creating happiness and peace. When we are organized, it often saves time and money and reduces unnecessary stress. There are many ways we can be more organized. Following are some simple ways (many of you may already be doing) that make future moments more enjoyable and less hectic.

- Shopping: Go grocery shopping weekly or fortnightly. Make a list of your meals and buy accordingly. Buy ripe and unripe fruit so that it lasts. Freeze enough milk and bread to last the week.

- Cooking: Cook two meals at once (e.g., when making spaghetti sauce, make enough for lasagne, or an extra spaghetti sauce) and freeze it. This means you can have easy nights, on Sunday, for example.

- Clothing: Keep your cupboard well organized. Prepare work clothes the night before (or once a week) so that you are not rushing to get ready in the morning.

- Holidays: Make a list of all you need so you can pack fast and easily. Have a designated place for important items to keep them safe and at hand.

- Gift box: Have a large box filled with gift cards, wrapping papers, ribbons, scissors, tape, and some gifts, so that you are always prepared, and in case you need a gift in a hurry.

- Daily Schedule: Mentally go through your day's activities to ensure you make the most of the day, maximizing your energy for work, fitness schedules, tasks, socializing, and rest.

- Diary Planning: As you make appointments days and weeks ahead of time, imagine how you will feel in these moments so you do not over-schedule or over-commit.

- Financial Preparation: Ensure you have adequate insurance, just in case of illness, car accident, theft, fire, injury, and much more. Having insurance offers some peace of mind for future moments.

- Finances: Work backward, budget, plan, save, set aside money to ensure you have enough when it is needed in your future moments.
- Be kind to your future self! Stress, pressure, fatigue, and even some illnesses can be avoided when we are kind to our future self.

Stress occurs when we rush, run late, criticize ourselves for forgetting things, are not prepared, are too busy, when we over-schedule, or when we do not fit exercise or relaxation into our lifestyle. We become fatigued and overwhelmed when we do not make time in our day for rest and "recharging our batteries." It is time consuming to keep popping down the street to buy groceries, and if we try on five outfits before work, we will most likely run late, adding to our anxiety. And who hasn't frantically run into a toy shop to buy a last-minute gift? All these stressors can be avoided in most cases by being kind to our future self, by planning our future moments. When we plan the future in the now, we enjoy many more moments.

Can you prepare your life, in advance, to ensure your future moments are gentle to you and enjoyable? Create opportunities for blessings galore by thinking about, "tasting," and preparing for your future moments.

Patience Is a Virtue

Have you ever thought, *I can't wait for this function to finish? I can't wait until the holidays? I just want this work day to be over?* Have you ever stood in a queue feeling frustrated, knowing you do not have time to wait? Ever felt your blood boiling in a traffic jam?

How often are you thinking, *I just want to get there? I just want to finish?* Do you feel like you are always in a hurry?

The reality is, we are always waiting. We are waiting to finish school, waiting to meet our life partner, waiting to have children. Then we wait for our children to go to school and survive their teenage years. We wait until we get "that promotion" and finish paying off the mortgage. We wait until we retire, and then we wait until we die. Life is waiting. We are always waiting for something.

As we can only live in this moment, we benefit by enjoying, savouring, and accepting *this* moment. It takes a real act of patience to accept that we need to enjoy life and accept our reality while we are *on* this journey, because we *never* really arrive until we die. Patience is enjoying the process. We benefit when we consciously enjoy the ride of life. The ride, this process of working toward our goals, this is our life! When we give power to each and every moment, when we see the sacredness in every detail, when we stop to smell the roses, when we stop placing more importance on a future moment and all our importance on the one moment we are living, in this second, then we have more power, more peace, and more happiness. Our life becomes so in focus, so colourful and intense. Inside every moment we have the potential to see magic. If we are angry, frustrated, and cursing the universe, we will miss the magic. The magic comes when we accept, embrace, and live each moment. In the present moment lies the sacredness of life. When we can be still, we hear the universe talking to us—through our bodies, our friends, our family, animals, and our souls.

If You Don't Believe, How Can You Achieve?

When you don't believe in yourself, how can anyone else? Whatever you want, your goals, personally and professionally, ask yourself if you really have faith that these goals will be achieved.

If you do not believe in yourself, you need to do the groundwork and reestablish faith in yourself.

Your attitude of self-belief is paramount to achieving your goals in life. Imagine for a moment that you are at a job interview, and you don't believe you are good enough to secure this job; you believe you have no hope in being offered this job. You would naturally become quiet and would not ask questions during the interview, hoping this "difficult" situation would quickly come to an end. To the person interviewing you, you would most likely appear disinterested, unenthusiastic, under-confident ... with perhaps some "negative vibe" the interviewer cannot put his or her finger on. These factors would impact his or her decision. However, if you believed you had a good chance of getting the job, you would appear more enthusiastic, as you would be asking questions, looking interested, and your chances of being offered the job would increase. *Your attitude affects the outcome.* Even when you are not talking, your attitude comes across very plainly! Your attitude directly influences your actions and body language, and as your attitude is part of the law of attraction, your attitude is pulling you toward your most dominant thought. Is that dominant thought, *I am a success,* or *I am a failure?* Well, if it is the latter, then please reread the section in chapter 2 about using affirmations to increase positive self-esteem. When you believe in yourself, almost anything is possible. When you believe almost anything is possible, then ... almost anything is possible!

If you want something, you need to make sure of two things: Do you believe you can achieve it? Do you actually want it? The universe responds to your soul's deepest desires and heartfelt beliefs, not just your actions.

Act As If

Regardless of what we do in life, from answering the telephone, doing something for the first time, working in a new career, or doing something we are afraid of, if we "act as if" we are confident, we are halfway to achieving this confidence. When you change the way you think about fear, it makes stressful events easier. Fear is your friend, not your enemy. The nervous beating heart and increased adrenaline are all part of the "magic" that helps improve your performance. When under pressure, your palms may sweat, your breathing may speed up, and you may feel full of energy. Work with these wonderful and helpful changes. Hide the signs of fear and nerves and enjoy the boost! So stand tall, or sit straight, hide your shaking hands, smile, take a deep breath, and silently thank your body for helping you. Your body is increasing blood flow to your brain, increasing your adrenalin, giving you increased energy and oxygen for peak performance and concentration.

When you look at the signs of nerves as your friend and become grateful, you can feel empowered rather than fearful. Even if you are terrified, feel the fear and move forward with confidence, knowing your nerves will give you an "edge." Whatever you are afraid of, imagine how hard this would be if you were half-asleep. Your body will ensure there is no chance of that. You are alert, ready for action, and ready to perform. Even if you don't feel this way, *act this way*, and it will eventually become natural to you. You can overcome fear—and go for your desires.

Often in life we need to exude a sense of calm, confidence, and poise. Even if we simply act calm, this will be calming for others and will help us remain calm. By projecting confidence, we appear confident.

Create Magical Memories

The future is a blank canvas, so why not sprinkle it with adventure? Adventure does not just happen by itself; we need to create these exciting moments; we need to plan a life for ourselves and our loved ones, filled with joy—this is our role. You may wish to please your soul by planning a concert experience, a trip to the cinema with friends, a wonderful holiday away, a fishing trip, or a night of entertaining friends or family. Life becomes exciting when we make it exciting. To look forward or back at life's special moments can give us great joy. If life was meant to be all work, there would be no weekends. And even if you love your work as much as I do, to enjoy life is to create exciting, magical, and memorable moments.

Often it is not entirely the doing that creates the most happiness but the anticipating. Create your own sparks of life as you constantly create a life for yourself, your family, and your friends filled with joyful experiences. Then when you are older, you can look back on your life, savouring the moments, having no regrets, because you took charge of your life. Plan it, do it, and savour the moments. How many exciting moments are you currently looking forward to over the next few weeks and months? Make a list of your exciting future moments. If there are not enough, start planning more.

Practice Daily Gratitude and Watch Your Life Transform

One day, while in a bookshop, I came across *The Simple Abundance Journal of Gratitude* by Sarah Ban Breathnach. I bought the book and began the practice of regularly making lists of all I was grateful for in my life. This is so powerful. In my book *Honeymooners Forever,* I encourage readers to stop criticizing and start praising.

I say that when we change from focusing on the negatives to focusing on the positives, we see so many more positives. The daily practice of being grateful for all the wonderful things in our life, from our bodies, our families, and our careers to the smallest of blessings, such as our food, our comfort, and shelter from the weather creates a firm foundation for even more blessings.

This is such a powerful activity that can make a huge and positive impact on our lives. So much so that I recommend to many of my clients that they pick five things each day to be grateful for. This is especially important for those suffering from depression, indecision, and trauma. Why wouldn't we want more blessings in our lives? Why wouldn't we want to see more good in our lives? It is so easy. We simply need to be thankful for the blessings we have, and the good in our life grows as if by magic!

Karma Is Real

Karma, a popular belief in Buddhism and Hinduism, is that your actions in this and previous lifetimes affect your current and future lives. Karma is a popular belief and incorporates two laws: the law of cause and effect, and the law of attraction. If you steal, you are likely to be robbed; if you are unfaithful, your partner is more likely to cheat on you; if you hit someone, you may be hit. Similarly, if you give to others, others will go out of their way to help you in return. Life is a constant flow of energy. Life is all about cycles, and even though terrible things happen to great people, if someone is selfish, uncaring, unsympathetic, and cruel, it is unlikely that great things will happen to him or her often. It is more than likely his or her life will be filled with more negative aspects than positive. We never really have to worry about retribution, in my opinion, as the universe has it all sorted out.

Change Is Part of Life

Life is an exciting journey, where only part is revealed along the way, and we can only see so far ahead. How do we get to true happiness and joy? How do we become in tune with the universe? We all benefit by *really* watching events unfold, analyzing what happens to us, and paying attention to what we *feel* like doing. What we want is real and *now*: we can't really say, "I want this one thing, and I will be happy" because our wants change. And while our partner may be the person we want our whole life, our jobs, homes, hobbies and visions change. Life is *about change*. We benefit when we accept change in our self, our partner, our family, and our life.

The Seven "Life Rules" from the Animal Kingdom

1. Love Unconditionally

A dog or cat gives you unconditional love, the kind of love that is so rare. When you walk in the door after a hard day's work, your dog is likely to greet you with 100 percent attention, wagging its tail and looking happy to see you. Yet in a human, that affection can be conditional, based on how busy the person is, what he or she may be thinking about at that time, or how the person feels about you that day. Your pets don't make these judgments—they just love you. The love from a dog is so wonderful! I use this example of a dog in my book *Honeymooners Forever*. I discuss how we could model our behaviour on a dog by how enthusiastically he greets his owner. Is your "tail wagging" when your partner walks in the door? Are you consistently greeting your partner with joy and happiness like your beautiful pet is greeting you?

2. Relax and Enjoy Life

A cat can lie in the sun for hours; a dog can go for a walk, relax, stretch, and snooze. They live a seemingly relaxed life. The human race and animals are so different. What do we humans do? We have schedules; we watch the time. We live with constant, harsh internal dialogue: *You need to get that report done faster. You are too slow. Hurry, no time for lunch ... just eat at your desk. Rest when you are finished.* I often watch my gorgeous dog, Cindy, as she spends time enjoying the sun and the gentle breeze, relaxing on a summer day. How often do you allow yourself to simply sit in the sun and enjoy the rays on your skin, as you enjoy a healthy, delicious lunch? How often do you think, *What can I do right now that will be relaxing or fun?* Life is not all work. When we rest, relax, and enjoy life, we become happier and more productive during our work time.

3. Live in the Moment

Have you ever seen a family pet sit and stress? They do not worry about bills, they do not constantly fret over past losses, and they do not worry tirelessly about future events. Their happiness, their simple joy, is profound. And it comes from acceptance of this moment, and from only living in the now. Our pets are a constant reminder that we need to slow down, be "present," and see the beauty and details in our lives. Many important messages, including messages from our bodies, our minds, and our universe, are easily missed when we are not living in this moment. Slow down and relax ... stop, smell the roses, and pat your pets!

4. Look Confident in the Face of Predators

I was talking with a friend who has spent a lot of time travelling. I asked her if she ever gets scared when travelling in a foreign country, and she replied that her attitude is so important. She said that when a rabbit bolts around, fearful and scared, the eagle, from high above in the air, has a greater chance of spotting that scared rabbit than the rabbits moving slowly. So if we as humans want to avoid being spotted and harassed or robbed by some of the less scrupulous humans on this planet, we can learn from the animal kingdom. We can move in a manner that does not attract attention. We can move with calmness, confidence, and as my friend said, with an attitude of no fear.

5. Use Your Instincts—Your Sixth Sense

It has been well documented that animals that are free to roam frequently escape dangerous tsunamis, volcanoes, and floods and survive. What gives animals forewarning of these upcoming events? Is it instinct? Is it a sixth sense? If a dog, cat, or snake can use their senses to avoid certain death, can we? Is it possible we have the same set of senses as animals but are not present enough to detect internal warnings? Is it due to our "racing brains" that we are not picking up signals of danger ahead? Or do we simply put any urges, inclinations, or feelings of danger out of our minds and argue the logical explanation against danger? We all have a sixth sense, and we can all use this to improve or even save our life. Life talks, and danger also talks; we need to be able to hear the warnings and act.

6. Animals Communicate with Us

Dogs seem to need no words, for they communicate with their bodies, eyes, walk, tails, looks, and in many cases, their bark. When we have spaghetti for dinner, I am positive my dog is silently communicating the words, "Give me some!" as she sits and peers at me with her huge eyes through our dining room window. That is our favourite meal, just as it seems to be her favourite meal. Similarly, when something is wrong, dogs seem to sense trouble, and in many cases, the humble family pet saves lives! We just need to look and listen.

Anita lived on a large country farm and had taken her two toddlers out of the house to go walk down the long driveway to check the mail. She forgot something, so she dashed inside. When she came back out of the farmhouse, she realized her youngest toddler had gone off and was nowhere to be seen. Knowing the house was surrounded by five dams, in different directions, Anita panicked. She simply did not know which way to run—if she ran the wrong way, her little girl could be drowned by the time she found her. The farm dog, Ben, had started to run in one direction before stopping and turning to look back to Anita. His face seemed to say, "Come on, this way." Anita rushed after him and soon found her little girl, lying in a shallow dam, on her back and covered in green slime. Anita quickly grabbed her, rushed her back to the house, and called the doctor. Her daughter was fine, but she had narrowly escaped drowning. Anita learned in that moment that the universe and animals often help us in a most magnificent way.

7.   We Communicate with Energy and Attitude

Growing up, I spent a lot of time working in our family business, dog-boarding kennels. We would have dogs of all different breeds, and my role was to feed them and clean kennels. I learned a lot about animals from this experience. I never once approached a dog in fear and was never bitten in anger. We had one visiting dog that would bark, snarl, and make every scary noise a dog could make, while baring her teeth. Most sane people would never enter this kennel with her, but I knew she was scared, and as long as I didn't get close to her, she would not attack. I also learned that in most cases, if you project no fear in your attitude, you will have the upper hand. (The exception, of course, is that if you go into a dog's backyard, you risk being attacked.) One day in my teens, as I was walking home, two German shepherd dogs ran toward me from their driveway. I instantly recognized that they needed to know I was boss. I yelled, "Go home!" and projected a "no fear; I am in charge" attitude and it worked like magic. They both stopped barking and retreated. While humans put great emphasis on words, animals put great emphasis on the energy and the attitude we give out.

Remain Detached to Gain Perspective

We humans are incredibly passionate, incredibly powerful, and we live lives that can be so dramatic—our energy fluctuates, our moods change, our hormones change. We may take stimulants like caffeine or depressants like alcohol, yet our goal is joy and relaxation. Ultimately we just don't want stress. Stress is so harmful. It is destructive to our relationships, our work, and our lives.

A technique you can use to de-stress yourself and to gain perspective and clarity about your life is to detach a little, to think about things from a different perspective. Instead of identifying with who you are and what you do, look at yourself as a spirit, in this body, in this lifetime. This is what you are doing, these are the roles you have, and these are your inspirations. If you believe in reincarnation, you'll have many lives, as you've already had many lives. This is your journey. When you pull back from the situation, when you are more analytical and less emotionally involved, you are more able to effectively run your life. Remaining a little detached from the process is a great way to relieve stress.

Many philosophers tell us of the power we have by understanding that we are a spirit in a body. Not one person will care in one hundred years about an argument we had or about one traumatic day at work. Stand back and analyze what happened, if anything goes wrong. Why did it happen? What can you learn from it? What are the positives? Then just remain detached. Notice your stress levels drop.

Homework—Are You Listening to The Rules?

1. Your past is talking to you: Do the personal history exercise involving your own history for work, relationships, houses, friends, etc. to discover more about your skills, needs, transitions, and future requirements.
2. Forward plan: Using the suggestions under Forward Planning, what changes can you make in your life to reduce stress and increase joy in your future moments?
3. Patience: What future moment is more important than now? How often do you find yourself feeling rushed to get to a

"future moment" instead of being fully present in this perfect moment right now?

4. Self-belief: In what areas of your life do you currently need to believe before you will succeed? Where do you have doubts? Make a list and use affirmations to increase beliefs.

5. Future: Make a list of all the future "memorable moments" you have created. If this list is short, plan more meaningful experiences for you and your loved ones to enjoy.

6. Be grateful daily: Practice being grateful for five things daily, and watch the positive impact on your attitude and your life. When we appreciate what we have, we feel a deeper sense of happiness, and by the law of attraction, more positives "show up" in our lives.

But there's another way of thinking about the world, which is ... pointed to by quantum mechanics, which suggested that the world is not this clockwork thing but more like an organism. It's a highly interconnected organismic thing ... which extends through space and time.—Dean Radin

When you have a desire, you are actually sending a message into the entire field—your slightest intention is rippling across the universe at the quantum level.—Deepak Chopra

CHAPTER 10

ARE YOU LISTENING TO THE UNIVERSE?

This book is about how the universe talks to us, how our universe conspires to help us. Often we don't realize that we are being helped until we look back with our spiritual eyes.

The Universe Tries to Help—We Just Need to Listen

Everything we experience is perception. One person views an event one way; another person views it another way. I believe strongly that the universe talks to us, is trying to teach us, reach out to us, help us, warn us, stop us, inspire us, and direct us with subtle forces, subtle energies, events, and experiences. Simply having the perception, the attitude that our world and the universe is "out to help us" is comforting, as is believing there is a deeper meaning to small or large events in our lives.

Leanne was driving along the same familiar road that she drove every work day, and she was forty five minutes away from her home. She grew annoyed at the car driving in front. It was

211

slowing down, speeding up, and driving a little erratically. Leanne was usually a patient woman, but she suddenly realized her indicator was on and she was about to turn around and go another way home. While this was not the usual way home, Leanne decided that if her "body" had just decided to go a different way, she would "go with it." Later that night she learned there had been a car accident and a fatality on the road she had avoided. The type of car involved was the exact make of car that Leanne had been following. Leanne may have avoided being involved in a fatal accident by listening to her body! Whether her guides, the universe, or her subconscious protected her from disaster, it manifested as "her body," indicating, turning and taking her on a safe route home.

The Universe Is Waiting to Serve You

The universe is like a plasticine ball, and we can create whatever we want from this ball. We don't create with our hands but with our thoughts. The universe is your sculpture, and with inspiration, planning, and hard work, you can achieve almost anything in life. Are you continually amazed by how incredible the universe is? How it delivers our dreams, sometimes late, sometimes in unexpected ways, but usually delivers? Whenever you want something, firmly plant this in your mind and then send the request to the universe. Don't worry about the details. Don't worry about how your dreams will happen; simply let the universe know your dreams.

We don't know what the future holds but the universe does. So when we have huge dreams, we need to work toward them, have faith, have passion, and leave it up to the universe to sort out the details.

The Universe Provides and Protects

Time after time, situation after situation, we see examples of how the universe has helped us. The examples are plentiful; we just don't spend time saying thank you to our universe.

So often I hear people stress about the future: "What if I lose my job? What if my spouse leaves me? What if I am left alone in this world?" We all have bad times, we all experience heartbreak, but the universe is not out to make us suffer. Everyone and everything is not out to get us. The universe is not a taker; I see the universe as a giver of love, as a huge hug. I see our universe as an unseen energy radiating throughout our world, and when we fall it reaches out to catch us. We still have terrible experiences, but the universe helps soften the blow. And by visualizing the universe in such a beautiful way, we eradicate common fears. Of course being aware of negative possibilities is important ... just try not to focus on them.

Stephen travelled overseas extensively, due to work. His wife booked the airline tickets and for some reason (that she was not aware of) she picked the top health cover insurance for the latest trip, which she had never picked before. Sadly, Stephen had a stroke in Europe. Due to having the top health cover insurance he was flown with a full medical crew, back to Australia, surrounded by doctors and nurses. Most associated expenses were covered. Thankfully, due to reasons that can't be explained, Stephen's wife could rest knowing her husband would be flown to Australia where they live, for further treatment, quickly and at minimal cost to the couple.

When you look for the ways in which you have been protected, saved, loved, and helped, you will see them. The universe is always watching, always waiting, to help you. You will still experience trauma and loss, yet the universe will help you heal.

Ask the Universe a Question

Many of us experience the wondrous power of thinking of a question and then the answer spontaneously is delivered, minutes or hours later. The answer may come as an advertisement on television, a friend may tell us the answer, or we may read about it in an article. This is the law of attraction, working magic in our lives. We are simply huge magnets; this proof is so evident (even amusing!) when we pose a question. We may wonder which model of car has best fuel economy, and a friend tells us all about their new low-cost, fuel-efficient car. We may start a health kick and find that our friends all start turning up to our home with different healthy options for morning tea, subtly showing us better ways to eat. Time and time again, the universe delivers our answers. Sometimes they are subtle, sometimes they are not. Can you see or hear them?

Defining Moments Shape Our Lives

In life, we have defining moments. These moments are powerful, memorable, and marked by huge decisions made in a split second. All of a sudden, as if out of nowhere, we feel certain about a decision—a change in our life, like a bolt of lightning has just hit us. A defining moment is an important decision that always feels 100 percent right at the time. Defining moments are powerful decisions that change our life direction, and they seem to "come to us" with certainty. They may relate to big changes in life (or small). The common elements are no indecision, no planning, and the decision feels like a breath of fresh air as it takes you on a new, exciting direction. A defining moment may be a decision to have another child, start a new hobby, join a gym, invest in property, retire, move house, end your relationship, book a holiday, change jobs, stop seeing a friend (as you no longer enjoy his or her company), spend more time with the family, embark on a new business venture, or stop a harmful addiction and transform your life. Think back over your life and pinpoint all of your defining moments that have shaped your life thus far.

Brad and Natasha lived in a beautiful home, but the street was busy and the area was not restful. They loved their home, so they had no plans to move. Then one day, the neighbours across the street had a violent, loud argument, and the police were called. It was very unsettling for Brad and Natasha. They called a real-estate company and made an appointment to view three houses in a quieter area, not far away, the following day. Brad and Natasha found their dream home, complete with bigger backyard in a more peaceful area, the next day. They moved in three months later. Brad and Natasha were lucky enough to find their dream home because they were sensitive to their feelings. As soon as their home no longer felt safe, peaceful, and enjoyable, they looked into other options. The defining moment for Brad and Natasha was instantly feeling a need for change on the day of the argument. They made a decision that defined their lives, and they made it within twenty-four hours.

When we have faith in our inner voice, and our snap decisions that "feel right," our direction in life may abruptly change, putting us on a different, much-improved path.

We Are Pupils and Teachers Will be Sent

When we are five years old we begin school, and usually we stay in school until we are eighteen. Some people go on to university, but it doesn't stop there. Our life is a school and we constantly learn new things. We are constantly seeking to improve. To improve, we also need to learn. To learn, we need teachers. Life is not like school, in that we sit in the classroom every day and the teachers stand in front of us and teach us maths, English, geography, and history. No, life is different. When we put out a need to the universe, whether it is an unconscious or conscious need, to learn something—the teacher appears. It is a beautiful and special thing.

Before I did the media campaign for my first book, *Honeymooners Forever*, I was scared. I had never dealt with the media before. I'd never appeared on a talk show before, and I was unsure how to work with this new medium. I was unsure how my life would change. A friend who worked in the media offered to help. She taught me all the facets that I needed to know, which helped me immensely. Since then, I've learned that whenever we need help, and we are ready to learn, the teachers will appear.

Coincidences Are Green or Red Lights in Life!

One of the most important messages our universe gives us is the coincidence. Coincidences are not merely things for us to comment on, to just stand back and say, "Wow! That was a coincidence." No way! The coincidences in our lives are the lights that light up the way. They are giving us one of two distinctively clear messages for our lives: stop or go.

Coincidences are an important way in which life talks to us. The more coincidences, the more life is talking, or the more we are listening. The more we listen and follow these coincidences, the more grounded we become, the more intuitive, and the more successful in love and life. When we listen to our inner voice, and when we keep an eye out for coincidences, we can have more confidence in our decision making. Coincidences, in most cases, will show us the way.

Coincidences also form part of the law of attraction, as the more focused we are on something, the more we will see this in our life. So coincidences incorporate life laws and messages, are powerful, and are not to be missed. When I need to make a decision, I look for the coincidences, and I do this almost daily. Nothing is too small to apply this to. Life (the universe) shows us what to do and what not to do. Obviously, we need to make decisions that are safe, in our best interests, and use our intuition. Coincidences light the path or put up a fence. Watch for these signs and for reasons to go ahead or to retreat. Your life will dramatically improve when you watch for and factor coincidences into your decision making. Do it daily if you can.

Life's Speed Bumps

There are no accidents in life; even small spills can mean a lot. There is often an important reason or message behind the negative events in our lives. From large to small, we need to try to decode these meanings. When we begin to listen to life, we can no longer drop a glass, watch it smash, and not look for the deeper meaning. Every little incident means so much. When you are grounded, when your energy is positive, you will seldom fall, drop things, or crash your car. When you are out of balance, you are more likely to be involved in accidents, slips, falls, and make mistakes. We are more likely to be involved in life's speed bumps when we are angry with ourselves and others, rushed, resentful, rebelling against life or someone, feeling stressed, frustrated, rushed, or like a victim. When we are resisting (not accepting) our situation, thoughts, or feelings, when it feels like everything is against us and we have no control, all these negatives affect our energy. This negative energy attracts negative events (the law of attraction), resulting in slips, falls, minor accidents, and in the worst case, serious accidents, such as car accidents. Next time you are running through the house and bump your elbow, stop to think about your thoughts. What were you just thinking?

The last time I rode my motorbike, I was feeling unhappy, as I was tired of spending almost every weekend motorbike riding with my family. All I really wanted to do was stay home, put my feet up, and have some quiet time. Well, I spent a few quiet hours in the hospital that day after falling off my motorbike no more than ten minutes into the ride. I was feeling rebellious, resentful, and annoyed, and my energy affected my riding. I ended up losing control and flying over the handlebars. I interpret this event as a lesson. We must be true to ourselves. If we do not want to participate, we must express our feelings to avoid possible accidents related to our unhappy and rebellious energy.

The Universe Has a Sense of Humour—Do You?

When we look for the humour in life, we find it! Just this past week, I saw an example of how the universe has a great sense of humour once again. My husband spent weeks making a huge wooden outdoor table for twelve people. We called this the "Viking table," as it has large wooden, crossed legs and is incredibly heavy, needing five men just to move it from the shed to the deck. For weeks we have been laughing about this Viking table, as it certainly won't blow away like the last one did. Last week I bought my husband a T-shirt/striped shirt combo. The T-shirt was covered by the striped shirt, and I assumed it was a plain black shirt. My husband wore his new shirt set, which looked great, and when it became too hot for the striped shirt, he removed it, revealing the unseen black T-shirt underneath. I started laughing hysterically. This new black T-shirt had one word printed on it: Viking, and the white face of a Viking. Incredible!

Some Universal Laws

The law of attraction—like attracts like (our thoughts create our reality).

The law of cause and effect—karma is real (if you steal, you are likely to be robbed).

The law of cycles—rhythm (why studying your personal history is so important).

The law of opposites—work in the up, rest in the down (blob time).

The law of motion—what starts in motion, stays in motion (spend at least 30 minutes a day on your goals).

The law of statistics—chance (don't risk it).

The law of physics—everything is energy starting with the mind (we need to visualize first).

The law of vibration—we are affected by each other's energy (remove yourself from angry energy).

There is one consciousness (Universal) and our mind is part of this one 'higher consciousness-collective consciousness' (inspirations—ask a question, receive an answer).

We are all entangled—we are not separate (what we do to another, we do to ourselves).

The Universe Is Talking to You

I am only writing this paragraph on my last day of writing. Why? Well, because if someone asked you to teach him or her how to walk, you would think it was easy. Yet because you do it *every* day without thinking, explaining how would take some thought. This is *the most important part of this book.* That is why I called the book *Are You Listening? Life Is Talking to YOU!*

I am convinced that every event in our life is connected, that coincidences show us the way. The universe is directing our days ever so subtly (and sometimes not so subtly!), and we benefit when we follow this gentle guidance. I asked the universe for a good example last night to write about in this paragraph, because although I have so many ways that the universe guides me, I just needed one. The example happened this morning.

I drove off in the morning eager to quickly go to the post office, and return home, as I had many hours of typing ahead. As I was approaching the post office, I was having a little debate in my mind whether I would drive the extra distance to buy petrol, or whether I would simply go to the post office and quickly return. I had decided that I would put "the book" first and forget about the petrol station. As I was about to make a U-turn into the post office car park, a car was closely following me, making a U-turn dangerous. I recognized in a second that this was the universe's subtle push, so I drove on to the petrol station. When I was in the petrol station, the mechanic noticed water leaking out of my car and he drove it straight into the workshop. He found the heater tap needed replacing. If I'd been stubborn and fought against the universe, I would have avoided going to the petrol station, and my car could have broken down on my four-hour drive the next day! I avoided this potential breakdown and I thank the universe. Yet I would not have been helped if I did not watch for the cues …

Be mindful that disappointments, delays, and cancellations could be in your best interest. If you are looking, you will see the ways in which the universe has saved you, helped you, and assisted you in your endeavours. When you are watching *every single day*, you will see the ways and read the subtle signs, and life *will* become easier. I know. How? I have been listening to the universe for many years now, and it helps me with everything from health, relationships, and career success to peace and organizing my life.

I wish you all the best that life has to offer! May you achieve your goals from this day on, as you look and listen carefully. May your love for yourself, and your life, deepen more daily.

Homework—Are You Listening to the Universe?

1. List all the ways the universe has helped you this past day, week, month, and year.
2. Think more deeply about coincidences. They will show you the way. The more you notice them, the more you will see, and the easier life will become. Life will seem less mysterious and more predictable!
3. Ask the universe a question and notice how the answer is delivered.
4. Life's slips: Next time you bump your elbow, almost have a car accident, or smash a glass, think about the thoughts and feelings you were experiencing at the time.
5. Try to see the funny side of your small setbacks and dramas. Heaven knows, the universe has a sense of humour, so don't be afraid to laugh at yourself. Laughter is good for the soul.
6. Next time an appointment is cancelled, traffic is jammed, you run late, or things don't go to plan, ask yourself: Could there be a deeper reason?

ABOUT THE AUTHOR

Phoebe Hutchison Dip Prof Counsellor (major relationships and conflict resolution, child development and effective parenting, grief and loss). Phoebe works as a relationship and crisis counsellor. She is a member of ACA—the Australian Counselling Association — and the Mental Health Professional Network. Phoebe's first book, published in 2007, is *Honeymooners Forever: Twelve Step Marriage Survival Guide* (Rekindle Publishing).

Her Australian morning television appearances include *Sunrise Breakfast Show with Kochie and Mel; 9am with David and Kim; Mornings with Kerri-Anne; Susie Elelman Morning Show;* and *Sri Lanka Today.* Phoebe's interviews have been published in the following magazines and newspapers and on the following websites: *That's Life* Magazine, *Good Health and Medicine* Magazine, *Herald Sun (Body & Soul), Frankston and Hastings Leader, Frankston Standard, Woman's Day Online* and *Women's Weekly Online.*

Phoebe is a happily married mother of two boys and lives in rural Victoria, Australia, with the cows, trees, and hills as neighbours. Her main priority in life is to enjoy daily peace and joy. Her life's passion is helping others live their best life.

For further information, please visit the author's websites:

www.phoebehutchison.com.au.

www.areyoulistening.com.au.

www.honeymoonersforever.com.au.

Acknowledgements

I would like to thank my husband and children, who have lovingly and patiently supported me in the writing of this book. A special thanks goes to my husband for always supporting me in the pursuit of my goals. Thank you to my wonderful parents and siblings for our beautiful relationships. Thank you to all my friends, in particular my friends Simone and Kylie, for your love.

Thank you to my wonderful Australian editor, Michelle Brown. You worked tirelessly on this book, to help me dig deeper with the writing of my ideas, and much more! We make a brilliant team. Sincere thanks goes to Jeff Peterson, my cartoonist, for being able to turn my ideas into fun and interesting cartoons. (You are a genius!) Thank you to the staff at Balboa Publishing for your patience, care, and enthusiasm shown while publishing this book.

I thank all the men and women who were interviewed for this book as case study examples. (All names and identifying details have been changed to protect the privacy of all involved.) I would like to thank all of my counselling clients. Without you, there would be no book. Through your challenges, I could identify what new therapies were needed, so I could create more. Your needs have inspired me to work harder to find answers and therapies for you—and for anyone else who is struggling with life.

Thank you, universe, for always guiding me, helping me, and loving me.

BIBLIOGRAPHY

Arntz, William and Chasse, Betsy and Vicente, Mark. *What the Bleep Do We know? Discovering the Endless Possibilities for Altering Your Everyday Reality.* Florida: Health Communications, Inc., 2005.

Ban Breathnach, Sarah. *Simple Abundance: A Daybook of Comfort and Joy.* New York: Warner Books, 2005.

Carnegie, Dale. *How to Win Friends & Influence People.* Sydney, Australia: Harper Collins Publishers, 1999.

Chopra, Deepak. *Ageless Body, Timeless Mind: A Practical Alternative to Growing Old.* London: Random House, 1993.

Chopra, Deepak. *Synchrodestiny: Harnessing the Infinite Power of Coincidence to Create Miracles.* London: Random House Group, 2005.

Coombes, Mitchell. *Sensing Spirit.* Pymble, Australia: Simon & Schuster (Australia) Pty Ltd., 2010.

De Becker, Gavin. *The Gift of Fear: Survival Signals that Protect Us from Violence.* New York: Dell Publishing a division of Random House, Inc., 1997.

Dyer, Dr Wayne. *Your Sacred Self: Making the Decision to be Free.* Sydney, NSW, Australia: Harper Collins Publishers, 1995.

Hartley-Brewer, Elizabeth. *Positive Parenting: Raising Children with Self-Esteem.* London: Ebury Press, 1994.

Hawkins, David. *Power vs. Force: The Hidden Determinants of Human Behaviour.* USA: Hay House, Inc., 2002.

Hay, Louise. *The Power Is within You:* Hay House Australia Pty. Ltd., 1991.

Hay, Louise. *You Can Heal Your Life:* Hay House Inc., 2002.

Hill, Napoleon. *Think and Grow Rich.* Rockville, Maryland, USA: Arc Manor, 2007.

Hougham, Paul. *The Atlas of Mind, Body, and Spirit.* London: Gaia Books, 2006.

Hutchison, Phoebe. *Honeymooners Forever: Twelve Step Marriage Survival Guide.* Melbourne, Australia: Rekindle Publishing, 2007.

Jeffers, Susan. *Feel the Fear ... and Do It Anyway.* London: Random House Group Ltd., 2007.

Jung, Carl. *Memories, Dreams, Reflections.* New York: Vintage Books, 1963.

Kübler-Ross, Elisabeth and Kessler, David. *On Grief and Grieving: Finding the Meaning of Grief Through the Five Stages of Loss.* New York: Scribner, 2005.

McCarthy, Paul. *8 Steps to a Remarkable Business: Innovative, Practical, and Affordable Ideas That Really Work.* Melbourne, Victoria, Australia: Business Support Network, 2005.

Noontil, Annette. *The Body is the Barometer of the soul II: So Be Your Own Doctor.* Kilsyth South, Victoria, Australia: Distributed by Brumby Books, 2008.

Peale, Norman Vincent. *The Power of Positive Thinking.* London: Mandarin Paperbacks, 1992.

Price, John Randolph. *The Superbeings.* Austin, Texas: Arnan IV Publishers, 1981.

Redfield, James. *The Celestine Prophecy.* Moorebank, NSW, Australia: Transworld Publishers (Australia) Pty Ltd., 1997.

Redfield, James. *The Celestine Vision: Living the New Spiritual Awareness.* New York: Warner Books, Inc., 1997.

Redfield, James. The Tenth Insight: Holding the Vision. Milsons Point, NSW, Australia: Transworld Publishers, 1999.

Sylver, Marshall. *Passion, Profit & Power:* Simon & Schuster, 1997.

Tolle, Eckhart. *A New Earth: Awakening to Your Life's Purpose.* Camberwell, Victoria, Australia: Penquin Group (Australia), 2005.

Tolle, Eckhart. *Stillness Speaks.* USA: New World Library, 2006.

Tolle, Eckhart. *The Power of Now: A Guide to Spiritual Enlightenment.* USA: New World Library and Namaste Publishing, 2004.

Tracy, Brian. *Maximum Achievement: Strategies and Skills That Will Unlock Your Hidden Powers to Succeed.* New York: Simon & Schuster Paperbacks, 1993.

Trump, Donald. *How to Get Rich: The Secrets of Business Success from the Star of the Apprentice.* Australia: Random House, Inc., 2005.

Trump, Donald with McIvor, Meredith. *Think Like a Billionaire: Everything You Need to Know About Success, Real Estate, and Life.* New York: Ballantine Books, 2005.

Walker, Lenore E. *The Battered Woman.* New York: Harper & Row Publishers, Inc., 1980.

Walsch, Neale Donald. *Conversations with God: An Uncommon Dialogue (Book 1).* New York: G.P. Putnam's Sons, a member of Penquin Putnam Inc., 1996.

Walsch, Neale Donald. *Questions and Answers on Conversations with God.* Virginia, USA: Hampton Roads Publishing Company, Inc., 1999.